The Report of the Committee of Enquiry into Children and Young People who Sexually Abuse Other Children

NCH

National Children's Home
Central Office, 85 Highbury Park, London N5 1UD
Telephone: 071-226 2033
Facsimile: 071-226 2537

Contents

Introduction

In recent years, interest and concern surrounding children and young people who sexually abuse other children has been growing. As more is learned from children who have been sexually abused about the perpetrators of that abuse, it is becoming increasingly clear that not only adults are involved, but teenagers and younger children too. A similar impression is gained from the retrospective accounts of adults who were abused as children. Staff in the National Children's Home have become increasingly aware of the problem, as have staff in other voluntary organisations and local authorities.

In spite of this growing level of awareness, little was known about the nature and causes of the sexually inappropriate behaviour of these youngsters, and even less about the long-term prospects of preventative treatment. However, the undoubted implications for child development and protection meant that this whole phenomenon could no longer be ignored or denied.

Firstly if, as seems to be the case with a large proportion of sex offences, the perpetrator is known to the victim and is frequently a family member or close associate, there is a need to ensure that further abuse does not take place. Secondly, if children or young people who abuse have been abused themselves, there is a need to work with their experience as a 'victim' as well as with their behaviour as a 'perpetrator'. Thirdly, current thinking suggests that recidivism is the norm in untreated sexual offenders, and that young male sexual abusers are likely to continue to sexually abuse unless help is offered in adolescence or earlier. In other words, it seems that in contrast to general delinquency, the young abuser is likely to grow into a pattern of sex offending rather than out of it, and there is a need for early intervention to prevent long-term addictive, abusive behaviour patterns developing.

Due to the relatively 'new' recognition of this situation and the very difficult nature of this type of abuse, as yet, no structured approach for intervention has been developed anywhere in the UK. In a research study undertaken by NCH on behalf of the Department of Health in 1990, it was revealed that under half of local authorities in England and Wales had any facilities to provide treatment for young sex abusers of children. Of those few facilities that did exist, most were very new, half had been established in the last five years and only two specialised to any extent in treatment work with young abusers. Although the effectiveness of intervention has yet to be established, many professionals who have encountered children or young people who have sexually abused other children have felt obliged to attempt some form of treatment work of their own.

So, whilst we knew that an increasing number of young abusers were coming to the attention of professionals, it was also becoming clear that there was a paucity of treatment facilities, no co-ordinated management structure for working with them and even a lack of clarity about the value and outcomes of intervention. Obviously this situation could not continue and as a result NCH took the decision to establish a Committee of Enquiry into Children and Young People who Sexually Abuse Other Children, and it is thanks to the interest and commitment of other voluntary organisations, The DoH and Home Office, plus concerned professionals from all over the UK that we are now able to present this report and its recommendations.

A lengthy process of consultation and research has enabled the Committee to make some clear statements about the need for an overall, systematic approach to be developed for dealing with cases where a child or young person has sexually abused another child. The Committee – in complete accordance with the recent Department of Health publication 'Working Together Under the Children Act 1989' – quite clearly sees this work being undertaken within the context of the Child Protection System, and special responsibilities are therefore implied for Area Child Protection Committees, whose specific function it would be to develop a strategic plan for working with young sex abusers.

In our conversations with professionals, the Committee have also been able to make some clear recommendations with regard to the urgent need for training and supervision for those working in the area. We also affirm the importance of further research to build on the current knowledge base and to help us to learn more about the impact of treatment work undertaken with young sex abusers.

Above all, the Committee hopes that its work will promote recognition of the 'problem' and lead to a greater legitimisation of the work; currently many professionals who are trying to work in this area do not believe that colleagues and managers support their involvement.

I am enormously grateful to the many professionals who shared their experiences with the Committee, and, of course, to the members of the Committee themselves who have worked so hard and given so much time over the last 15 months. I am grateful to the Department of Health and its Social Services Inspectorate and to the Home Office for the participation of their representatives as observers. I know all members of the Committee will join me in expressing our particular thanks to Cathy Cooper and Jan van Wagtendonk of NCH who co-ordinated the work of the Committee. Their dedication, hard work and leadership is very much appreciated.

Our hope is that this report will prove helpful to all who have responsibility in providing services for children and young people who sexually abuse other children – those in Central Government, those at policy level in social service, health, probation and police departments, as well as those working at practitioner level. We hope our report and recommendations will focus attention and provide a way forward in an area which deserves not only serious consideration, but urgent action.

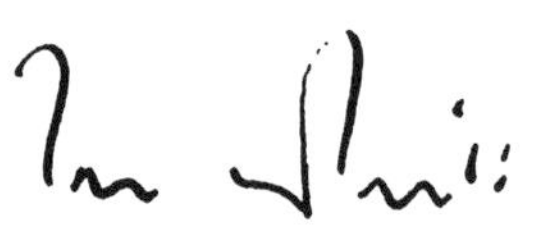

Tom White CBE
NCH Chief Executive

Members of the Committee

ARNON BENTOVIM	Consultant Child Psychiatrist, Great Ormond Street and Tavistock Clinic
IRENE BLOOMFIELD	Project Leader, Pole Park Family Centre, Dundee
ANN DOYLE	Rainer Foundation
DAVID GLASGOW	Lecturer, Forensic Clinical Psychology, Liverpool University and Ashworth Special Hospital
VALERIE HOWARTH	Executive Director, ChildLine
PHILIP NOYES	Director of Public Policy, NSPCC (resigned from Committee 16.7.91)
JENNIFER TEMKIN	Professor of Law, University of Buckingham
EILEEN VIZARD	Consultant Child Psychiatrist, Tavistock Clinic
TOM WHITE (Chair)	Chief Executive, NCH
DAVID WILLIAMS	Detective Sergeant, New Scotland Yard

Observers:

ROSEMARY ARKLEY	Social Services Inspectorate
RUPERT HUGHES	Department of Health
SUSAN WILLMINGTON	Home Office, Probation Service Division

Secretariat:

CATHY COOPER	Assistant Policy Officer, NCH
JAN VAN WAGTENDONK	National Development Consultant Child Sexual Abuse, NCH

Chapter 1: Background

1.1 In October 1990, a Committee of Enquiry was established, funded by NCH, to look into the whole issue of children and young people under the age of 18 who sexually abuse other children.

The terms of reference of the Committee were as follows:

1. To investigate the problem of children and young people under 18 years of age who sexually abuse other children, having regard to:

a) Known incidence
b) Extent of existing treatment facilities
c) The management of case investigation
d) Appropriate forms of intervention to change and/or modify behaviour
e) Appropriate management processes needed to maximise effective services.

2. To make recommendations.

1.2 The membership of the Committee attempted to reflect the range of professional disciplines currently working in this area.

1.3 In order to complete its work, the Committee embarked upon an extensive information gathering exercise attempting to draw upon the knowledge and experiences of any professionals who had worked with young abusers. This process had six major strands:

1.3.1 *A series of 3 regional consultations held in London, Leeds and Glasgow.* The purpose of these events was to enable those with knowledge and experience to share something of their work, discuss issues of concern, and raise questions about the work and the context in which it is undertaken. Open invitations were sent through appropriate networks, and a total of around 150 professionals attended the three consultations. The consultations were based on small group sessions in which participants were encouraged to share their work experience, and the particular issues of direct concern to them. A broad range of professions were represented, indicating that the issue of young abusers is one which impinges upon the work, and is coming to the attention of staff in several different settings. The largest proportion of staff who attended came from a social work background, although they represented various work situations; some were residential social workers, some were specialist child abuse officers, some were based in local social work teams, some were involved in juvenile justice projects. A large number of clinicians also attended; psychologists, psychiatrists, paediatricians, health visitors. Some came from a probation background, some were social researchers involved directly or indirectly in related programmes of research, and some were policy or development officers. Those who attended also represented a good range of practitioners and managers from the statutory, voluntary and private sectors, and they were based in a variety of residential and community settings. Some participants had direct experience of working with young abusers, and are currently involved in ongoing multi-disciplinary treatment programmes. Others are working in relative isolation, responding to a need as best they can because there is no other available treatment option. Many had come to the consultations from the perspective of wanting to learn, because they were becoming aware of cases but felt unprepared and unable to deal with them. All, however, were in little doubt that there is a situation in existence which has until the present day been largely ignored, and that there are a substantial number of young people who have been involved in abusive behaviour who need to be worked with in a constructive way.

1.3.2 *A series of 3 national consultations in London.* From the regional consultations, it became evident that concerns and issues raised fell broadly into three main areas:

- Issues surrounding work with young abusers in residential and day care settings.
- Issues surrounding clinical work.
- Legal, Policy and Management Issues.

Three further consultations were organised to explore these areas in more detail. Unlike the regional consultations, these seminars were organised by invitation only, and specific professionals with relevant experience were targeted.

1.3.3 *A general call for information through the professional and academic press.*

1.3.4 *A meeting with representatives of the Regional Offenders Treatment Association (ROTA)*[1]. As some members of ROTA had experience of working with young people who have abused, it was felt important to link in with their network. Consequently, a meeting was held between representatives of ROTA and representatives of the Committee of Enquiry in order to discuss issues of concern to both groups, and possible ways forward.

1.3.5 *A research study*, funded by the DoH, looking in detail at the working of a sample of 16 facilities currently engaged in the treatment of young sex abusers (see Appendix 1).

1.3.6 *A meeting with independent researchers*. The Committee recognised that, in addition to its own research, several other researchers were currently engaged in research in this field, or had recently been involved in such research. An open meeting was held for those researchers with an interest, to share their research experience and results with the Committee.

1.4 The following report draws heavily upon information and opinions gathered during this consultative process. The Committee of Enquiry have attempted, where relevant and possible, to propose recommendations for the future development of this work. Whilst the recommendations are those of the Committee, they are based, to a large extent upon the ideas and practical experience of those who participated in and contributed towards the process of information gathering described above.

1.5 The Committee recognises the dilemma which exists with regard to terminology. Various terms are currently used when referring to children and young people who are known to have abused, or are believed to have abused other children. The most widely used terms are 'perpetrator', 'offender', and 'abuser.' Whilst the Committee has made certain decisions about the ways in which these terms will be used in the context of this report, it recognises the need for continued debate on this issue. Such a debate must take into account the different professional and national contexts in which work with young sex abusers takes place.

1.6 *For consistency, the expression 'children and young people who sexually abuse' is the general term of reference used in the report. However, it is recognised that several other terms might be equally, if not more acceptable in certain contexts, and the terms 'offender', 'abuser' and 'perpetrator' have also been used to varying degrees. Where the term 'offender' has been used, the reference is specifically to a young person who has been through a criminal investigation and who has either been convicted of a sexual offence or has admitted a sexual offence and has received a caution, or other non-court action. Where the term 'abuser' has been used the reference is to a child or young person who was clearly aware of his actions, planned the incident and understands the abusive nature of the act. The term 'perpetrator', in general usage, covers both the term 'abuser' and the term 'offender', and has been used as an alternative, more general form to either offender, or abuser. Where none of these terms appear suitable, the child or young person has been referred to as one who has displayed 'sexually inappropriate' or 'sexualised' behaviour patterns.*

Chapter 2: What is Abusive Behaviour?

2.1. Whilst the consultative process indicated that most professionals involved in the area are fairly clear what they believe to be abusive behaviour, it is very difficult to present an all inclusive 'hard and fast' definition which precisely and unambiguously distinguishes between those behaviours which are abusive, and those which are merely inappropriate. At both extremes of the spectrum, there appears to be little problem in recognising the nature of the behaviours concerned. Those behaviours which cause definitional ambiguity are those which are 'on the borderline'.

2.2 As will be discussed in later chapters, there is concern that much abusive behaviour perpetrated by children and young people is going unchallenged and unrecognised because those involved with children are denying the significance of the behaviours they are seeing, or are being told about. The boundary between what is abusive and what is part of normal childhood or youthful experimentation is quite blurred. There is no generally agreed understanding of what constitutes an abusive act when perpetrated by a child or young person because there is no generally agreed understanding of what normal sexual development is. Is what some adults might regard as 'sexually abusive behaviour', in fact, normal childhood exploration about differences between the sexes? How much sexual knowledge do children have, at what ages, and how do existing power structures in society influence children's behaviour towards one another? It is clear that we do not as yet know enough about this aspect to be clear in our judgments although recent studies have been undertaken in an attempt to illuminate thinking in this area[1]. The issue of defining when a child or young person is abusing is therefore fraught with problems.

2.3 **From discussions which took place during the consultative process, however, the Committee does believe that there is a way forward in terms of reaching agreed understandings with regard to abusive behaviour perpetrated by young people. The Committee believes that the significance of particular behaviours needs to be explored with special regard to the related concepts of true consent, power imbalance, and exploitation. In trying to determine what is abusive behaviour and what is not, these ideas are crucial. The Committee believes that the absence of true consent, and the presence of a power imbalance and exploitation are common to *all* experiences of abuse.**

2.4 'True consent' is not necessarily the same as legal consent. Where there is a truly consenting relationship (even if it is against the law), this may not be abusive, and is therefore outside the scope of any management and intervention programme aimed at dealing with abusive behaviour. **In this regard, true consent should be thought of as being *informed, not forced, in an equal relationship, without financial or other inducements, and free of any pressure to comply.*** An example of true consent conflicting with legal consent could be found in the situation of two young men who have received sentences for homosexual consensual sex. The discrepancy in the age of consent for homosexual and heterosexual acts leads to situations whereby, for example, an act between two truly consenting 16 year old boys is against the law, but is not abusive.

2.5 Other diverse situations demonstrate how a lack of true consent (as defined above) creates an abusive situation. For example, the case of the seven-year-old girl who is sexually abusing a seventeen-year-old girl who has a disability; or the eight-year-old girl who is 'acting out' her own abuse by interfering with her four-year-old brother in sexual play – she warns him that she will tell their mother that he has been naughty if he does not join in her 'games'.

2.6 Crucial to the notion of true consent is the equality of the relationship. Any factor which makes a relationship unequal creates a power imbalance; and in assessing the nature of any particular behaviour, it is essential to look at the social relationship between those involved. Power imbalances can obviously occur through differences in age, size, levels of sexual knowledge or understanding, or developmental level. Race and gender can also be significant in this regard, as can be the factor of whether or not one party has learning difficulties. As a rough guide, there would be great concern if the age difference between the two young people was more than two years. If the (alleged) abuser is post pubertal and the 'victim' pre-pubertal, there is also cause for concern. The greater the age difference, the more likely it is that abuse has occurred. If the perceived 'victim' has a learning disability or other communication problems, which mean that they cannot easily give consent, cannot easily recognise abuse, or cannot easily communicate to another person that they have been abused, then the act may well be abusive.

2.7 If the act took place within the context of an authority relationship such as babysitting or scout leadership it is indicative of the exploitation of a power imbalance and is therefore likely to be abusive. Whilst the absence of exploitation does not necessarily mean that the nature of the relationship is legitimate, the presence of such exploitation is much more likely to be indicative of abuse.

2.8 In order to more fully determine the nature of the incident, and the levels of true consent, power imbalance and exploitation involved, the Committee believes that there are certain indicators which can be looked for; certain questions which can be asked in order to obtain a clearer picture of the incident. The following questions point towards those features which the Committee believe to be significant in determining whether or not an act is abusive.

- *What is the nature of the relationship between the 'perpetrator' and the 'victim'?* Does one party have authority over the other, and what other power differentials are present?
- *Does the incident involve acts which have sexual implications through physical actions involving sexual parts of the body, or the use of sexual language which is offensive or which makes explicit sexual suggestions?*
- *How sophisticated is the activity?* Is the type of sexual activity age appropriate? If it is not, and it shows 'excessive sexual knowledge' or there appear to be age-inappropriate sexual motivations in the actions of the perpetrator, then the act is more likely to be abusive.
- *How often, and for how long did the activity happen?* Whilst it is acknowledged that one short incident may be abusive, frequency and persistence are strong indicators of abuse.
- *Has a pattern of activity changed over time?* Has it become more frequent, severe or deviant. Are 'victims' getting younger? An evolving pattern of behaviour can be suggestive of abuse.
- *Is there overt aggression, coercion or bribery?* If so, this usually indicates an abusive relationship.
- *What is the experience of the person who has been 'abused'?* Were the behaviours perceived by the recipient as abusive, or is the recipient blaming him/herself for what happened? Either scenario indicates that the act may have been abusive.
- *Have there been any attempts to secure secrecy by any of the individuals involved?* If there have, then the reasons for this need to be clarified.
- *How was the activity revealed?* Was there a disclosure from either the 'abuser' or the 'victim', or was the behaviour 'discovered' or disclosed after an inadvertent comment?
- *Does the 'abuser' appear to target a particular type of 'victim'?* Common features such as age, sex, or vulnerability may suggest a target group, which is indicative of abuse.
- *What are the nature of any fantasies?* Those with fantasies which include abusive scenarios are, perhaps, more likely to express these in abusive situations. Fantasies give a clue to self-image, views about sex and the nature of the sexual interest .

2.9 Whilst none of these factors are definitive or prescriptive – they are *indicators* – the presence of one or more of them should alert the professional to the fact that something is going on which ought to raise concern and which needs to be investigated in more detail. The answers to the questions may enable the professional to determine an appropriate course of action to be taken, where there is concern that abuse has taken place. If an act appears to be inappropriate, but not abusive, there may still be a need for some kind of behaviour management or intervention (especially if the act has taken place within a residential setting), although the nature of this intervention would probably be very different from that suited to an act which was definitely abusive in nature.

2.10 ***Where there is concern that a child or young person has been involved in sexually abusive behaviour, the Committee would recommend that this should be brought to the attention of either the Social Services or the Police, and that an investigation should be undertaken.*** Any subsequent assessment of the case would then need to look more closely at the nature of the incident.

Chapter 3: Overview of Current Situation

Incidence

3.1 The latest annual Home Office figures (1989) report that of all offenders cautioned or found guilty of sex offences, 32% were under the age of 21 and 17% were under the age of 16[1].

3.2 However, it is not possible to rely on these 'official' figures to present an accurate picture of the incidence of cases of sexual abuse which involve a child or young person as the perpetrator. In fact, the systematic collection of accurate national statistics remains a virtual impossibility. Problems in collecting accurate data arise for three main reasons:

3.2.1 Many incidents of abuse (regardless of age of perpetrator) go unreported or unrecorded. Children and young people can find it exceedingly difficult to disclose what is happening to them; feelings of guilt are often prominent, and sometimes threats will have been used against the victim to prevent them talking. Sometimes children feel they have to 'put up with things', bullying for instance, which they have come to believe is a 'normal' childhood experience. If children and young people were enabled to report abusive experiences, and were affirmed in doing so, a much higher incidence might well emerge. Even when a disclosure *is* made to a friend or family member, there can be denial or disbelief on the part of the person to whom the disclosure is made, and the child who is being/has been abused may be discouraged from talking more widely about the abuse. Even if the social services or police are involved, there may be insufficient evidence to corroborate the story. Consequently, no charge will be made against the abuser, and no retrievable record kept of the incident (although Social Services may have an informal record). In England and Wales, children under the age of ten are exempt from criminal liability anyway, as are children under the age of eight in Scotland.

3.2.2 Denial and minimisation of the significance of abuse perpetrated by children and young people is also common among parents, police officers and other professionals. Many behaviours are put down to 'adolescent experimentation' when other people might well choose to define them as being abusive. This attitude also reduces the number of incidents which are reported and which eventually lead to convictions. It also leads to great inconsistencies between different areas of the country in terms of dealing with children and young people who abuse, because of the possible range of reactions towards this behaviour; what happens in one place may not happen in another, and in terms of collecting accurate incidence figures this is problematic. Even when a caution is made, the record of the offence may not be indicative of the severity of the abusive behaviour.

3.2.3 Many incidents which are recognised are not dealt with through the criminal justice system possibly because the young person concerned is already in the care of a local authority, and the events took place some time prior to the disclosure/discovery of abuse. Outside the criminal justice system, there is no formal collection of data which takes account of the age of a perpetrator of sexual abuse.

3.3 There are clearly major obstacles in the path of gathering accurate, national figures, and these will not be overcome until there is greater comprehension and recognition of the significance of children's sexually abusive behaviour, and until more established guidelines and structures are in place to enable professionals to respond in a consistent and appropriate way.

3.4 However, in spite of all these difficulties in collecting accurate national statistics, a variety of research studies have been able to provide some information about the proportion of abuse which is perpetrated by children and young people. The results display a striking level of consistency. Finkelhor (1979)[2] in his retrospective survey of adults concerning abusive experiences in childhood reported that 33.6% of those who abused girls, and 39.1% of those who abused boys, were between the ages of 10 and 19. In a recent study of sexual abuse investigations in Liverpool (1989-1990) Horne et al[3] found that 34.4% of allegations involved children or young persons abusing another child or young person. The age range of alleged abusers was from below 7 to 17 years of age, with 35% of abusers in the 8-12 year category and 59% in the 13-17 year category. Hengeller (1989)[4] estimated that 36% of child sexual abuse cases involved a juvenile perpetrator, and the Northern Ireland Child Sexual Abuse Study[5] carried out between January and December 1987 concluded that in a sample of 408 established cases of sexual abuse, 36.1% involved a teenage perpetrator. One very recent study – an exploratory study of the prevalence of sexual abuse in a sample of 16-21 year olds conducted by the Child Abuse Studies Unit at the Polytechnic of North London[6] – concluded that 28% of cases of sexual abuse involved a perpetrator under the age of 18. In 15% of those cases (4.2% of cases overall) the perpetrator was known to be a female.

3.5 Monck, Bentovim, Goodall et al in another recently completed study[7] indicated that 15%-20% of cases of within-family abuse involve a child or young person as the perpetrator. Whilst this is a lower rate, the study excluded cases of extra-familial abuse. The studies mentioned in 3.4 included such cases. It is possible that children and young people are more likely to be responsible for abuse outside the family, for example within the social peer group setting.

Investigation, Referral and Assessment

Investigation

3.6 From the consultation sessions, it became clear that very few areas of the country have a consistent, co-ordinated approach to this type of investigation. It was felt that joint investigation frequently falls down when a child or young person is alleged as the perpetrator. Agencies sometimes investigate on their own and without reference to appropriate professionals or organisations. Depending on the route referral takes, decisions are often made about disposal (by, for example, some police or staff in schools or residential establishments) without reference to professionals who are involved in child sexual abuse work, or who have specialist knowledge of sexually abusive behaviour.

3.7 It is acknowledged that co-ordination between agencies is, in any circumstances, difficult to achieve. A range of pragmatic considerations conspire against such an arrangement. However, where incidents of children and young people abusing other children are concerned, additional factors appear to come into play. A lack of co-ordinated approach may be due to denial of the seriousness of sexually abusive behaviour, the difficulty of obtaining conclusive evidence, an embarrassment about dealing with sexual issues, a lack of formal guidance on how to deal with these matters, and/or belief systems which support the idea that the child or young person will 'grow out of it' and would suffer by being labelled as an abuser or sex offender. As has been discussed above, such attitudes lead to unreliable incidence figures, and a lack of resources for those children or young people who have abused other children.

Referral

3.8 There are indications that referrals are made reluctantly, both by the general public and professionals. This is true with regard to referrals for investigation to the Police and Social Services, and referrals for assessment and treatment to Social Services, Health Authorities, Child and Family Psychiatry clinics, or other specialist facilities.

3.9 Often, owing to denial and other factors, management is reluctant to devote resources to this work. The general public and other professionals have little knowledge about how to recognise and deal with sexualised behaviour; those who do recognise the need to refer a case for specialist assistance may not be aware of what facilities are available. Even where the problem is not entirely denied it is accorded a low priority, and agency managers may still be reluctant to devote resources in order to provide appropriate services.

3.10 Referrals to specialist facilities which have been established to work with adolescent abusers seem to depend on i) the potential referrers having knowledge of the facility, and ii) the status of the facility. Some have built up direct relationships with social work departments and the courts, and receive referrals from these sources. However, most arrangements are ad hoc and do not reflect an agreed system of dealing with the problem in its entirety. There are very few co-ordinated referral systems. In Shropshire, however, a system has been developed in relation to dealing with young people who have been involved with sexually abusive behaviour towards other adolescents. Following police investigation, referrals are made to a special project through the Juvenile Liaison Panel. Referrals are also accepted from social workers and residential workers who are worried about the sexualised behaviour of children or young people in care. A three-stage process is then put in motion involving:

- A pre-assessment report to the Juvenile Liaison Meeting, or a child protection conference, outlining the views of the offender, the views of the parents/carers, and the school. It would also include an initial assessment of risk.
- An assessment after 6 to 8 sessions with the young person. This takes account of family history, attitudes to offences, sexual history, knowledge, experience and fantasies, denials, excuses, minimisations, and general attitudes about sexuality. Future risk assessment is also undertaken.
- Long-term treatment/therapy, if appropriate.

Such a system (which is described in more detail in Appendix 1) has allowed a more co-ordinated response to work with adolescents, and has led locally to changes in attitude to the needs of adolescents who commit sexual offences. The system is one example of an agency which has tried to tackle a real problem, and to find a way forward. Although this particular model has now been superceded by that proposed in 'Working Together' (1991)[8], many of the processes involved in it remain of value, and the system has certainly served to highlight the need for an overall co-ordinated, multi-agency response to deal with the referral and assessment of children and young people who abuse other children.

Assessment

3.11 All those involved in working with young abusers emphasise the need for careful assessment prior to embarking on a treatment programme. One possible model for the assessment process, including the proposed content of an assessment, is outlined in Chapter 5.37 to 5.44.

Treatment: The Management and Intervention Process

3.12 Even if it is not possible to determine precisely the rate of incidence of children and young people who abuse, it is clear that concern surrounding the situation is well grounded. It is this very real and genuine concern from many professionals – arising out of an increasing awareness that around one third of all cases of sexual abuse may involve a *young* abuser – which has led to the development of a range of different types of work with young abusers. Such work is, however, still sparse and is dependent upon appropriate referrals being made in the first place. Those agencies which have responded appear to have done so largely as a result of the awareness and commitment of certain staff (ie, staff recognised a 'problem' and felt it necessary to respond in some way). Obviously, the availability of resources and appropriate facilities has also been an enabling factor in those areas where work has proceeded. However, some 'treatment projects' have developed on the bare minimum of resources, and out of the goodwill of staff who are prepared to work in their own time, or with no specific specialist back up. Different models of work with different age groups have developed, in different settings and with varying degrees of structure .

3.13 The NCH/DoH Survey of Treatment Facilities for Young Sexual Abusers of Children (1990)[9] indicated that the majority of those with whom work was undertaken were males aged between 15 and 17. The vast majority of those who attended the Committee's consultative seminars, and who were working with young abusers, were working with abusers in the 15 to 18 age range. It appears, therefore, that where structured 'treatment' work is being undertaken, it is largely with this older group. However, in the NCH/DoH survey, 23% of facilities reported doing occasional work with boys under the age of nine, who were involved with what were seen as sexually victimising or sexually-inappropriate behaviours with other children. Work with younger children, described in the consultative seminars, tended to be either individual play therapy or work undertaken in a residential care setting where staff talked to the children and set limits on their behaviour through negative sanctions. Clearly, staff are aware of the need to determine age-appropriate responses.

3.14 In spite of the recent finding from a study conducted by the Child Abuse Studies Unit at the Polytechnic of North London[10] that 4.2% of cases of child abuse involved a female perpetrator, virtually no female abusers were reported to be seen by any facility in the NCH/DoH survey. The Committee of Enquiry's consultative process did however involve very few staff who were working with young female abusers.

3.15 The NCH/DoH survey did identify five different types of treatment facilities which appear to have developed some work with children and young people who abuse. These are:

- non-hospital based clinics (eg, child guidance clinics),
- hospital-based clinics,
- special groups,
- community-based facilities/family centres,
- residential facilities.

3.16 Appendix 2 provides a summary of a recently completed research report, carried out on behalf of the Committee of Enquiry. This research describes in some detail the treatment offered by a range of facilities which have developed work with children and young people who abuse other children, and provides a thorough overview of the types of project which have emerged.

3.17 One important issue the Committee of Enquiry had to take into account was whether or not it is appropriate to talk about 'treatment' in relation to children and young people who sexually abuse. Certainly, in the field of working with adult sexual offenders the idea of treatment, with the implication that there is a 'cure' and that the offender has an illness which is outside his control, has been rejected by many practitioners, who prefer to talk about 'management' of sex offenders and 'intervention'. Similarly, practitioners working with adolescent sex offenders are worried about the use of the term 'treatment' and would prefer to use 'management' and 'intervention'. Whether the same can be said for those working with younger children who show sexualised behaviour patterns is in some doubt; for those younger children, their behaviour pattern may well be changed by intervention, with an extinguishing of sexually abusive behaviour and sexually abusive arousal. **While the Committee recognises that the term 'treatment' is widely used, and has a status within the legal context, it feels that terms such as 'management' and 'intervention' are appropriate and valuable in this work, and that their use should be encouraged.**

What is the need for Management and Intervention and Treatment?

3.18 It appears that young sex offenders may be an exception to what has been called the 'new orthodoxy' within the juvenile justice field. A report from NACRO on the DHSS Intermediate Treatment Initiative to Divert Juvenile Offenders from Care and Custody (1991)[11] has stated that:

"the principles underlying the new orthodoxy have enjoyed increasingly widespread adherence among professionals involved in dealing with juvenile crime".

These principles see that:

"responses to delinquency by social services and other welfare agencies can have unintended and unhelpful consequences for juvenile offenders. Formal interventions should therefore be avoided wherever possible and their intrusiveness kept to a minimum."

Such a philosophy implies a general acceptance of the view that the majority of young offenders will naturally move away from offending behaviour as they become older.

3.19 However, Vizard (1991)[12] and others have taken the view that this philosophy does not necessarily hold true for young sex abusers. Whilst it is believed that most juvenile offenders grow out of offending behaviour as part of a general maturational process, there is evidence to suggest that abusing adolescents grow into a pattern of sexually abusive behaviour. In a study by Abel et al (1987)[13], it was found that 53% of adults known to have 'molested' male children reported arousal to young males by the age of 15, and 59% of adult sex offenders reported the onset of offending behaviour during adolescence.

3.20 Research does not indicate what proportion of young people who have sexually abused go on to become adult abusers, nor does it indicate what factors would inhibit or encourage such a process. It seems fair to assume that some will not go on to become abusers while others will. However, the consultation exercise did reveal that a large number of professionals believe that without informed and child-centred intervention, young people who sexually abuse are likely to continue their sexually abusive behaviour patterns, particularly where such abuse was a part of the young person's sexual and masturbatory fantasies. In addition, there is strong evidence to suggest that most sexually abusive behaviour is pre-planned by the abuser. A minority of those attending the consultative seminars argued that intervention can have negative effects, and actually further the process to becoming an adult offender; it was felt that a young person could be labelled for life, and that intervention itself may confirm the young person in a belief that they are 'deviant'. **On balance, and bearing these points in mind, the Committee feels that there is a need for intervention, but that such intervention should be planned, informed, child-centred and thoroughly evaluated.**

Management and Intervention Programmes

3.21 This is a new and emerging field, and a number of different intervention approaches have been developed and are currently in use in various projects in the UK. Before discussing issues relating to interventions with children and young people who have sexually abused other children, it may be of value to summarise the categories within which most interventions fall. The following does not claim to be an exhaustive list, nor definitive of the interventions:

- Interventions designed to contain an immediate risk; these could involve removal of the abuser from the situation in which sexual abuse took place, or increased supervision in the situation in which it took place. Obviously these responses are short-term, and partial.

- Interventions designed to assess and/or modify behaviour. These could include observation of the child or young person in their living environment, psycho-educational approaches, or therapeutic management approaches.

Psycho-educational approaches

3.22 These include formal sex education, social relationship education, and modelling of appropriate sexual and non-sexual peer relationships. This work could also take place within the natural living environment, if that environment were conducive to such an approach; for example, psycho-educational approaches combined with family therapy or work with residential care staff or foster carers could ensure that a child or young person receives appropriate help. The psycho-educational approach could also be undertaken within a group work setting using male and female co-therapists, and could involve training in peer relationships using social skills training. The latter tends to be undertaken in all male group settings, although often with male and female co-therapists. The involvement of family members in this work, particularly when the child or young person is living at home, or is likely to return home, is seen as vital. Family members need information about the implications of sexually abusive behaviour, the need for intervention to avoid such behaviour becoming a pattern, the aims of intervention, what intervention will entail, and information in general about sexual development, attitudes and beliefs, and how they can help the child or young person. The support of family members can be crucial in determining the co-operation of the child or young person in the treatment process, and thus in its' outcome.

Therapeutic Management approaches

3.23 These would include:

- Approaches which analyze the cycle of the sexually abusive behaviour of the child or young person.
- Approaches which attempt to reduce denial (which is often a major component of both assessment and intervention aimed at bringing about change) through focused individual work, or facilitating the challenging of denial and group work.
- Approaches which attempt to investigate a child or young person's own abusive experiences within the context of their own abusive behaviour.
- Approaches which attempt to increase empathy with the victim. This is a significant component of individual and group work, and is intended to enable the abuser to understand the significance of their acts and to respond more appropriately in the future.
- Approaches which attempt a modification of those cognitions which are believed to increase and maintain sexually abusive behaviour. This can take place through education or in direct conversation, but is more systematically addressed by cognitive behaviour modification techniques.
- Approaches which include individual or group psycho-therapeutic techniques to put the abusive behaviour into a general context.
- Approaches which specifically attempt to prevent relapse into the sexually abusive behaviour.
- Approaches which are aimed at managing anger.
- Approaches which attempt to modify behaviour. Behaviour Modification[14] in its narrow definition is now rarely used on its own; however, it is often adopted where problem behaviours are displayed by children, or by those who have learning difficulties. It is likely to be more significant where a child of limited verbal ability, through age or learning difficulty, is engaging in sexually inappropriate behaviour. More loosely defined, the modification of risky or pre-offence behaviours is a significant component of relapse prevention packages. Modification of patterns of sexual interest involves cognitive behavioural techniques aimed at shaping a risky or unacceptable sexual interest into a less risky, more acceptable form. Monitoring, analyzing, and assessing sexual interest may be through self-report, but some workers may also use physiological measures of arousal, including erection. The Committee believes that physiological measures should only be used in exceptional circumstances, these being where a young person approaching adulthood poses a serious risk of committing further offences, where the use of such methods is carefully planned and part of a systematic intervention programme, and where the possible negative consequences of its use have been carefully considered. Use of such methods should also only take place within clear procedural and ethical guidelines (see Chapter 5.75 - 5.77).

3.23.1 **The Committee wishes to express concern about methods which make use of sexually explicit materials in an ad hoc and unsystematic way, and which cannot be justified as part of the assessment or treatment process. In this context, 'sexually explicit material' should be taken to include official documentation such as child protection conference minutes or police statements, assessment questionnaires, audio tape material designed to assess and change sexual arousal, visual material, and commercially available and legal audio, visual and written material.**

3.23.2 The use of some sexually explicit material may be useful in the treatment process. For example, material which a young person has already used for his own sexual gratification, or which is presented by the young person as fantasy or personal experience. It is also acknowledged that some *new* material may be presented by other young abusers in the groupwork process. ***The Committee commends to all professionals the statement on the use of sexually explicit material in work with adult sex offenders, as developed by ROTA***[15], *but recommends that even more care should be taken in work with young abusers. The Committee endorses the view of ROTA that all sexually explicit material*

"to a greater or lesser extent .... can be misused, leading to further abuse, offences and negative role modelling. It is therefore essential that in using any sexually explicit material, practitioners are clear why and how it is being used, and that it (the work) is set in the context of the underlying sexual and social attitudes and power relationships of men towards women and children."[16]

3.24 The above approaches can occur in any combination, and may take place in various settings. The setting for the programme will depend on the assessment of risk vis à vis the child or young person. Settings therefore may be Young Offender Institutions (preferably with specialist facilities), Youth Treatment Centres and Aycliffe Centre for Children, Secure Accommodation in Local Authority control, non-secure residential facilities, hospital settings and community settings.

3.25 Although common aspects of treatment programmes are identified in all work, the individual needs of the child or young person must be taken into consideration. It is also important to see the sexual abuse in the context of the whole life experience of the child or young person. Indeed, a fundamental starting point for all work in this area must be that children and young people are children and young people first, and that sexually abusive behaviour is a problem they have; it is dangerous to see these children and young people only as offenders or abusers. It must also be taken into account that children and young people are at different stages of development.

3.26 The goals of adult and adolescent or child treatment programmes may be similar, but the context and means adopted to achieve these goals need to be quite distinct. Work with children and/or young people must be informed by well established techniques, and practices for working must take into account the young person's immature, but developing personality and sexuality. There needs to be less reliance on verbal and conceptual techniques, and a greater emphasis on education and activity based work including painting, drawing, games and drama.

3.27 Ryan (1988)[17], working in the USA, has developed a consensus statement for the National Adolescent Perpetrators Network, which encompasses the following:

- Adolescent sex offenders must be held accountable for their inappropriate sexual acts.
- They must receive 'sex offence specific' treatment, rather than treatment which focuses in a general sense on meeting their needs in terms of appropriate care.
- The treatment mode of choice is a peer group setting with individual, behavioural and family treatment as an adjunct.
- Certain risk assessment criteria can help determine the relative safety of choosing an out-patient approach in the community, as opposed to a residential placement.
- Treatment of the young person should cover identifiable areas and the programme should be described in detail. The programme should address the issue of the abusive behaviour pattern. It should also look at how to reverse and create more benign patterns, and at normative data on sexual development. In addition, social skills training, anger control and diversion, development of empathy, dealing with own abuse and victimisation should all be addressed.
- Court involvement is an asset which can facilitate engagement and the follow through of treatment.

3.28 This consensus statement is to a large extent replicated in the UK. The Committee of Enquiry holds the view that most professionals who are involved in direct work would accept that their work contains the elements mentioned above.

3.29 At this stage, no evaluative data is available which identifies the essential characteristics of successful intervention programmes, not least because these require evaluation as part of a longitudinal research programme which has yet to be undertaken. However, it would be possible to measure changes in the short-term with respect to those factors which may have an influence on longer term offending behaviour, for example changes in cognitive distortions, victim empathy, inappropriate arousal, parental support and attitudes, employment and school performance, social skills, and self esteem. The measurement of such changes would enable information to be gathered about which methods are successful with which kind of offender/abuser. National comparisons could be made, and such information will be vital in long-term planning for resources (for further discussion of this issue see Chapter 7).

3.30 A major question surrounding management and intervention programmes is one of time scale. Can such programmes be contained in 10-12 sessions of group work, or in one year of work, or is a longer timescale needed? Current experience suggests that intervention may well need to be long-term rather than short-term. Much will depend on the assessment of risk and history of sexualised behaviour.

3.31 Little information has been forthcoming about work with children below the age of 10-12. None of the group work programmes about which the Committee learned included younger children in their work, but pre-pubescent children obviously raise different issues. What is their understanding of their own behaviour? What understanding do they have of sexuality? To what extent can such children be held responsible for their behaviour, if at all?

3.32 One suggestion put to the Committee encompasses the notion that with increasing age there is an increase in personal responsibility and a corresponding decrease in parent/carer responsibility. If considered in these terms, a younger child's sexualised behaviour patterns and the control of that behaviour to keep the child safe must lie with a responsible adult. Although parental/carer attitudes to a child/young person are always important, and such persons should be part of the treatment programme and their needs addressed, this is even more vital in work with younger children. There is one North American programme for working with younger children who show sexualised behaviour patterns, which is called SPARK (Support Programme for Abuse Reactive Kids) – developed by Kee McFarlane and Carolyn Cunningham[18]. This programme is aimed at 5-12 year-olds and includes a work programme that can be adjusted to the age and developmental level of the child. The programme uses as its base, a cognitive behavioural approach and includes social skills training. The Committee is not aware of any specific programmes developed for this age group in the UK. Most of those who contributed to the consultations saw children in this age group as children who had been sexualised by traumatic experiences. It was seen as important to ensure that help be given for any abusive experience the child may have had, as well as for any abusive behaviours displayed.

3.33 All management and intervention programmes must take account of power and gender issues. Sexual abuse does not occur in a vacuum; the norms and values of society play a large part in this area of work. It is important to make a connection between what are often described as 'cognitive distortions' (beliefs held by abusers which permit, facilitate, maintain or justify sexually abusive behaviour – see Chapter 3.59) and their origins in inappropriate messages relating to sexuality, power and gender communicated to children through the family, peers, role models and the media (see Chapter 5.9 - 5.15). Techniques such as 'Its a Man's World'[19] and 'Grapevine'[20] are used to highlight these phenomena.

3.34 In addition, any assessment and management of this work needs to be culturally sensitive. The consultations revealed a strong feeling that work in this area is culturally narrow and does not take adequate account of ethnic and cultural backgrounds. Most of those who attended the consultations were working with white young offenders, and some belief existed that whilst white young sex offenders receive treatment, black young sex offenders are dealt with more punitively. Indeed, there is evidence of racial bias in the criminal justice system[21], and there is no indication to suggest that this situation is any different where work with young sex offenders is concerned.

3.35 Efforts to reduce the future probability of a child or young person becoming involved in sexually abusive behaviour attempt to enhance the young person's:

- intellectual understanding of the impact and consequences of abusive behaviour;
- ability to empathise with the experience of victims;
- ability to recognise and modify any fantasies which are likely to render abusive behaviour more probable;
- ability to recognise and avoid behaviour patterns which are likely to render abusive behaviour more probable;
- ability to recognise and avoid situations which have, in the past, been antecedents of abusive behaviour;
- ability to recognise and modify thoughts ('thinking errors' or cognitions) which i) impair or limit any or all of the above abilities, and/or ii) have been antecedents of abuse in the past;
- ability to implement an appropriate prepared and rehearsed strategy upon recognition of the possibility of the imminent development of an abusive situation.

3.36 It is crucial to understand that the needs of a particular child or young person are likely to vary with circumstances and developmental level. The above enhancements are not significantly different from those sought during adult treatment programmes, but the *degree* to which they are sought in a given child may be age dependent. For example, it would be entirely inappropriate and unethical to attempt to elicit and modify sexual fantasies in a prepubertal child whose abusive behaviour was not related to the presence of such fantasies. Even in circumstances in which a need to achieve one of the above is clearly present, the manner in which it is achieved must be developmentally appropriate. Group discussion of the impact of abuse is appropriate with older children, whereas younger children are more likely to benefit from carefully structured and educative play, utilising age appropriate materials. Similarly, the actual expression of the goal is likely to vary with age and development. An appropriate strategy for a young child who recognises the imminence of abusive behaviour might be to seek the assistance and guidance of a particular parent or carer. An older child, enjoying correspondingly more autonomy is likely to be required to implement a more complex strategy of behaviour and cognitions which are designed to avert the potential occurrence of sexual abuse.

3.37 In describing all the above factors, difficulties do emerge in the consideration of management and intervention programmes, and these should be borne in mind:

- at present, no training or membership of any profession necessarily enables an individual to work with sexual offenders, let alone children or young people who sexually abuse;
- the needs of children vary so much with age, ability and circumstances that it is most unlikely that any single course of training could cover the entire spectrum of needs;
- children or young people are likely to abuse other children as a result of many interacting factors which must be addressed in different situations and at different levels;
- formal knowledge and research pertaining to child sexual abuse in general, and, in particular, that perpetrated by children or young people, is drawn from a range of disciplines;
- the range of responses to acts of sexual abuse perpetrated by children or young people is considerable and may be undertaken by a variety of professionals.

Children and Young People who Abuse in Residential Care

3.38 Recent media exposures have highlighted some of the very real dangers involved in the existing system of residential and institutional care. Whilst there is a great deal of commitment and skilled intervention from the vast majority of staff in the residential sector, there are risks which it is virtually impossible to eradicate. As with any area of work in which adults have close and continuous interaction with children and young people, residential child care settings – in which there will be many children who are particularly vulnerable because abuse will have already become an integral part of their personal history – are likely to attract those individuals who might seek to take advantage of the position of responsibility and authority in which they are placed. There is also the difficulty of some children and young people being susceptible to engaging in abusive behaviour with other children or young people. La Fontaine (1991)[22], for example, has noted that many calls taken through ChildLine's 'Bullying' helpline were from children living in residential care who appeared to be actually experiencing sexual harassment or abuse. A dilemma exists surrounding the whole issue of the placement of abusing children in residential care, alongside other non-abusing youngsters, some of whom may have previously been abused. Where non-abusing and abusing children and young people are placed in the same environment, there is automatically conflict between the rights of non-abusing children or young people and the rights of the children and young people who have abused. Particular concerns were raised throughout the consultative process about the placement of children and young people who abuse in a residential setting. These concerns focused, in particular, around the safety and rights of other, possibly abused, young people residing in the same establishment.

3.39 Whilst some residential therapeutic communities operate a policy whereby all residents know why the other residents are placed there (including their abusive behaviour), in many others the abusive behaviour is not openly acknowledged and the young people are allowed to develop a 'cover story'. Where treatment is taking place in a residential environment (eg, in a secure unit, assessment centre, treatment unit, or residential school) and where cover stories are allowed to develop, the cover story can interfere with the treatment as the young person may come to believe their own cover story rather than acknowledging the real reason for their stay in the establishment.

3.40 Powerful dilemmas are raised by the issues of cover stories. For carers of children and young people who abuse, it is often difficult to contemplate total openness about what the child or young person has done. There are fears that the child or young person will be 'scapegoated', ousted by their peer group, or violently attacked. Some carers believe that such children or young people should be allowed to keep the details of their offending behaviour confidential, and that information should only be disclosed with consent. On the other hand, many of those who care for children and young people who have been abused, and who are not sexually abusive themselves, feel that the youngsters in their care need to have the information about the abusive behaviour of other children in order to protect themselves against abuse. Many believe that non-abusing children should not be placed at all in an environment where there are children and young people who are known to have sexually abused other children in the past.

3.41 Undoubtedly, these conflicting points of view create a dilemma, and this dilemma should not be underestimated. It is not in the interests of any child or young person to be placed in a situation where they may be abused, and neither is it in the best interests of an abusing child or young person to be in an environment where they are physically attacked or threatened or isolated from their peer group. This issue is further addressed in Chapter 5.53 - 5.65 where specific recommendations are made concerning the placement in residential care of children and young people who abuse other children.

3.42 There is a trend within the field of juvenile delinquency and child care in general, towards working in a community setting, rather than a residential one. Whilst there is obviously an issue around the appropriateness of working with young abusers in a residential setting, there remains a strong body of opinion which advocates the need for a residential setting in the case of some children and young people (either those who have themselves been abused *or* those who have abused others). Such a setting is seen as being able to provide the necessary intensity of therapeutic work, as well as a role of containment. Indeed, an assessment may well conclude that the level of dangerousness presented by a child or young person is such that a secure, residential (yet therapeutic) environment, is the only realistic option.

3.43 Whilst the decision between residential or community placement for a young abuser is linked to the degree of risk involved to other children, there is an issue about the extent to which certain residential facilities are equipped and suitably prepared to be able to constructively manage these cases. Certainly staff working in residential establishments who participated in the consultations were worried about dealing with overt sexualised behaviour when they had little information or guidance as to how to deal with it, nor access to facilities to which a young person could be referred for more specialised treatment. Staff also reported experiencing difficulties in dealing with their own feelings and sexuality when encountering children and young people who are involved in sexually abusive behaviour. In many cases, all staff felt able to do was increase vigilance, without directly dealing with the situation; obviously this situation has not been therapeutic for the youngsters, and it has not provided the staff with an opportunity to work through and confront their own feelings. Neither has it been able to prevent further incidences of children and young people in some residential homes being abused by other residents.

Children and Young People who Abuse in Foster care

3.44 Most of the considerations expressed in the above paragraphs on residential care also apply to foster care, and there is little doubt that foster carers are often confronted with the problem of children or young people sexually abusing others. Most of the time, such situations occur when an abused child 'acts out' his/her own abuse with other children. This is often the first indication that a child has been abused. A substantial proportion of children who need to be placed with foster carers have been sexually abused. Consequently, many foster workers believe that all foster carers should be made fully aware of what this might mean in terms of the behaviour of their foster child.

Theoretical Contributions

3.45 This section describes some of the noteworthy theoretical contributions which have been made in relation to the issues of causation and intervention with children and young people who abuse other children. The contributions are selected from a rapidly increasing literature on child sexual abuse, and children and young people who abuse other children. The accounts are intended to be brief descriptions of the particular contributions, not critical appraisals. More complete accounts of each of the theoretical contributions can be found in the original literature.

3.46 The theories described below are not exhaustive, and the Committee is not advocating any one particular understanding. The Committee recognises that there is no single factor which causes children and young people to abuse others; such behaviours always follow a complex interaction between a number of factors.

3.47 The following theoretical ideas will be described:

- Pre-conditions for abuse
- Traumagenic dynamics
- Cycle of Abuse
- Post Traumatic Stress Disorder
- Addiction
- Societal Factors
- Cognitive Distortions

It is acknowledged that some of these ideas will overlap, or even, in places, be contradictory. Again, it must be emphasised that at this time, there is no one theory of causation which is universally agreed.

3.48 Finkelhor, one of the foremost researchers in the area of child sexual abuse, has developed a structure for thinking about child sexual abuse which forms a very useful starting point[23]. His work – developed within the context of intervention with adult offenders – points to four *pre-conditions which must exist for sexual abuse to occur.* These are:

- the abuser must have a motivation to sexually abuse,
- the abuser must overcome internal inhibitions to abuse,
- the abuser must overcome external inhibitions to abuse,
- the abuser must overcome the child's inhibitions.

3.49 In his work, Finkelhor analyses these four pre-conditions, citing a number of causative, or contributory factors from a variety of theoretical standpoints, and analyzes them from a societal and an individual perspective.

3.50 In other work undertaken by Finkelhor and Browne (1986)[24] the notion of *Traumagenic Dynamics* is developed. This describes responses to abuse under four headings:

Traumatic Sexualisation

3.50.1 Traumatic sexualisation occurs when a child is sexually abused. Such abuse 'rewards' and reinforces inappropriate sexual behaviour and inappropriate sexual responses. Alternatively, it may lead children to avoid situations which remind them of the abuse, or to replay the abusive events. Children may experience flashbacks of abusive acts and the fears associated with them. They may become pre-occupied with sexual thoughts and behaviour which may lead on to their own re-abuse, or may lead them to sexually abuse other children; the child's sexually abusive experience may lead to the sexualisation of closeness and intimate relationships and/or the sexualisation of power.

Powerlessness

3.50.2 Powerlessness occurs as a result of the invasion of the body which the child experiences during abuse. This invasion can lead to a strong sense of vulnerability, a feeling of not being protected, strong fears, and a sense of helplessness. This may lead to the child being in a constant state of fear and anxiety, and a feeling that they are not able to control anything that happens to them. Such a psychological state may lead to learning difficulties, and/or a sense of despair; alternatively it can express itself in a need to control and dominate events and people. It may also lead to aggressive abusive behaviour.

Betrayal

3.50.3 Betrayal can occur in situations where the abuser is someone in whom the child has placed trust. In the course of the abuse, that trust is blatantly exploited, and this is likely to leave the child or young person feeling confused and lacking in trust. A common reaction to this is for the young person to enter into new, intense relationships which do not last, but which create feelings of disappointment, loneliness, and disillusion. These feelings can, in turn, lead to hostility, angry distrust, retaliation and anti-social behaviour.

Stigmatisation

3.50.4 Stigmatisation occurs when an abused child or young person is blamed for any problems which arise from the abuse eg, separation of parents, unemployment, financial difficulties. Often, abused children feel guilty, and blame themselves for what has happened. They can come to believe that they are 'bad', and this can lead to a sense of isolation. In addition, if a child or young person comes to believe that they are to blame, and that they are a dangerous person to know, they may well seek to engage in behaviours which 'prove' this; such behaviours may include aggressive sexualised behaviour.

3.51 The *Cycle of Abuse* is often cited as a major contributory factor in the development of abusive behaviour. At its simplest, this refers to a child or young person abusing other children as a consequence of his or her own abuse and sexual victimisation. Toni Cavanagh Johnson indicates in her research on female sexual abusers[25], that *all* had suffered sexual abuse in their own childhood. This is however, a small scale study, and it appears to the Committee that at this stage, not enough is known of the etiology of female abusers to be able to draw any conclusions. More research on this subject is needed, particularly in view of the Kelly Study[26] which indicated that 15% of sexual abuse committed by those under the age of 18 involved young female abusers. (The Committee is not aware of any projects working with young women abusers and very few professionals indicated that they undertook such work). Research on adolescent boys and adult abusers would indicate a range of between 32% and 50% who indicate having suffered sexual abuse in their past[27]. This notion of a 'cycle of abuse' should not be confused with the idea of a 'sexual assault cycle' proposed by Gail Ryan[28] which is discussed more fully in section 3.60.

3.52 It appears that for some children and young people, the need to cope with their own abuse may well lead to a denial of having been abused at all (through the use of such interpretations as 'I enjoyed it' or 'I initiated it') in order to feel in control. For others, it may lead to an identification with the aggressor, and an acting out of the abuse with themselves in the role of the abuser, controlling events. For younger children, acting out what they have learned is often seen as a sign that they have been abused.

3.53 It must be emphasised however, that as far as is known, the vast majority of children or young people who have been abused themselves *do not* go on to abuse others. It is not known at this stage what factors are involved in influencing whether or not someone who has been abused goes on to abuse others; only the development of a comprehensive, research programme would be able to begin to contribute to this particular area of knowledge. However, sexually abusive behaviour patterns cannot simply be explained as a way of acting out previous sexual abuse; they may also be a result of other forms of previous abuse.

3.54 It is frequently suggested that children and young people who have experienced abuse may suffer from *Post Traumatic Stress Disorder* (PTSD) as a consequence[29]. PTSD is associated with serious traumatic events. Symptoms are described as re-experiencing the trauma in dreams, recurrent images and thoughts, a general sense of numbness and feelings of not being involved in the real world, guilt at having survived, sleep disturbance, and an exaggerated, startled response[30]. In some circumstances, sexually abusive behaviour may be a response to the trauma of having been abused.

3.55 Sexualised behaviour is often described as being *addictive*. There is no doubt that sexual arousal and orgasm are powerful reinforcers of behaviour, and such reinforcement can occur as a result of actual behaviour, or fantasised behaviour. In this way, the child or young person can become dependant upon sexual fantasy or behaviour, which can be described as an addiction. Carnes (1983) describes the following signs of addiction in sexuality:

- pre-occupation with sex or sexual thoughts
- ritualisation of sexuality
- an element of compulsivity
- keeping the sexual activity and thoughts secret
- a pain relieving quality to the sexual activity
- the sexual activity takes place outside of a caring relationship
- feelings of despair and shame
- the activity increases in intensity and frequency
- denial of the activities or thoughts

3.56 Any assessment would need to test out the extent to which such an addiction has been formed for a child or young person.

3.57 Not all abusing children or young people have been previously abused themselves. The *societal tolerance* of male dominance, the role of women, stereotypical relationships, and power hierarchies are seen as significant in reinforcing sexually abusive behaviour. The relatively free availability of pornography, attitudes to male aggression (such as 'boys will be boys'), and tolerance of abusive behaviour committed whilst under the influence of alcohol, all combine to present young males with the idea that young women or girls have no right to refuse men anything. This, and other cognitions lead to a legitimisation of physical and sexual violence towards women, including abuse by young men of women and children.

3.58 Coupled with the idea that children can be sexually seductive (or precocious) – which is a similar cognitive distortion sanctioned by society – these views can be powerful reinforcers of sexually abusive behaviour. The idea that a young person's experience of sexual failure in relationships with peers can lead to the development of sexual relationships with children who can be controlled and manipulated, needs to be understood within the context of those societal factors described above.

3.59 A further theoretical understanding is that which forms the basis of many treatment/intervention programmes, both in this country, and in the USA. This understanding is based on the idea that *cognitive distortions*, or 'thinking errors' are fundamental in the maintenance of abusive behaviour. The underlying theoretical framework has been developed by (among others) Howard Goldstein[31]. The basic concepts of this theory can be summarised as follows:

- people can best be understood as searching for, and moving towards their own goals,
- people construct their own versions of reality through what they have learned,
- people gain certainty in their lives by 'adaptation'; a process which enables them to manage the outside world,
- adaptation is influenced by our concept of ourselves, and how that affects our perceptions.

3.60 Certain intervention programmes aim to make young people aware of their thinking errors in such a way that if they are to continue with their abusive behaviour they do so having made a clear, conscious, deliberate choice. The work will involve a detailed analysis of what Gail Ryan has described as a 'sexual assault cycle'[32]. Such a cycle provides a framework within the treatment programme for abusers to understand factors in their offending behaviour. The young person is enabled to identify thoughts and feelings involved in the abuse process, and is confronted with his thinking errors, and presented with alternative ways of thinking.

3.61 The final theoretical understanding to be presented here relates to the development of sexually inappropriate behaviour in children and young people with learning disabilities. The Committee has become aware of a very few professionals who are working with children or young people with learning disabilities, who have become involved in sexually inappropriate behaviours. It is known that sexual development in people with mild or moderate learning disabilities follows the 'normal' pattern[33], and there is often a general failure to recognise that young people with learning disabilities have the same feelings, desires, and expectations as other young people. There is often a failure to recognise the right of young people with learning disabilities to have satisfying sexual relationships. It is also known that some people with learning disabilities do express themselves sexually in ways which are socially inappropriate[34]. Inappropriate sexual behaviour can therefore be seen as the result of a lack of sex education and/or a lack of opportunity to express sexuality.

Chapter 4: Legal Considerations

The Need for a Mandate

4.1 A major issue raised during the consultative process was that of the need for a legal mandate to work with young perpetrators of sexual abuse. The debate focused on whether management, intervention and treatment could be successful without obtaining a legal mandate from the courts, either through criminal or civil proceedings. Those who favoured a legal mandate through prosecuting the young abuser believed it would have the following advantages:

- It would ensure that both the victim and the perpetrator are aware of society's condemnation of the behaviour;
- It would ensure that everyone takes the issue seriously;
- It would ensure that the young person would receive some treatment or intervention;
- It would strengthen the chances of the young person remaining involved in the treatment/intervention process.

4.2 Those opposed, or doubtful, about the usefulness of a legal mandate obtained through prosecution felt that it was too 'risky'. The prosecution could well fail, for example through lack of evidence or because the victim was a poor witness, thus providing the young defendant with an excuse for not facing up to and dealing with his behaviour. The danger of labelling a young person as a sex offender was also raised, and some professionals had objections to mandated intervention in general. Furthermore, a general policy of prosecuting young sex abusers would be contrary to current juvenile justice philosophy and practice which favour using prosecution as a last resort (see Chapter 3.18).

4.3 On the other hand, there are indications, particularly from the USA, that in the case of adult sex offenders, if treatment or intervention is not legally mandated, those involved opt out and many do not complete the full programme. A similar picture emerged from the consultations, practitioners reporting a higher drop out rate when working with young people who were not under a court order to attend a programme. The Regional Offender Treatment Association (ROTA)[1] indicated in its submission to the Committee that the weaker the mandate, the weaker the young person's commitment to the work is likely to be. The recommendation of ROTA was to secure a legal mandate wherever possible. Others, however, would argue that such a philosophy would make facilities inflexible, discourage self-referral or referral originated by a parent or carer, and could delay the treatment process. The alternative to a mandate obtained through the criminal courts is one obtained through civil proceedings. The possibilities for this are discussed below. However, without any legal mandate – criminal or civil – it would be essential for parents to have a high involvement and commitment to ensure that treatment is sustained. Where parents or carers are not supportive, the chances are that the intervention will be resisted. Given current levels of denial, it may well be difficult to ensure parental/carer support for this work.

4.4 **The Committee believes that intervention programmes must be available on both a legally mandated and 'voluntary' basis. A decision regarding which is the most appropriate course of action to take should be made on the basis of an assessment of the child or young person, which takes all circumstances into account (see chapter 5.44).**

4.5 In some cases, the seriousness of the offence may indicate a clear need for immediate intervention. However, if the situation is at all unclear, the police should delay making a decision until the circumstances have been clarified. In order for an informed decision to be made about the best way forward for each particular young person, an assessment should take place of the level of commitment of the young person and his/her family to a treatment process. In Scotland, this decision must be made within 104 days.

The Role of the Legal System in Intervention

4.6 The differences in approach between the Child Protection System and the Juvenile Justice System are referred to in more detail in the following paragraphs. It is clear however, that either system may be used to obtain treatment for a young person, although the child protection system is certainly more appropriate for younger children, given the age of criminal responsibility in England and Wales (10 years) and Scotland (8 years). The choice of which system to use will require careful consideration based on an assessment of the case.

Civil Procedures

4.7 The Children Act 1989 does not appear to have addressed itself specifically to the problem of children and young people who abuse other children. However, its new structures do suggest certain possibilities in England and Wales for facilitating intervention in this context.

4.8 Schedule 2 of the Act obliges local authorities to take reasonable steps, both to encourage juveniles not to commit offences, and to reduce the need to bring criminal proceedings against juveniles in their area. This should enable local authorities, in conjunction with other relevant agencies, to establish programmes which are specifically designed for children and young people who have been involved in sexually abusive behaviour. Under Section 17 of the Act, Local Authorities are required to make available advice, guidance and counselling to 'children in need' while they are living at home with their families; however one might otherwise categorise sexually abusive children, they could certainly be defined as 'children in need'. Such action would inevitably have resource implications for local authorities.

4.9 If the support and co-operation of the child's family is absent, or the home situation is a contributory factor in the overall situation, proceedings for a care or supervision order might need to be considered. Under the Act, it is no longer possible to make any order in such proceedings simply on the basis that a child has committed an offence. Under Section 31, in order to make a care order, it is necessary to show that the child is suffering, or is likely to suffer significant harm, and that this is due either to *'the care given to the child or likely to be given to him if the order were not made, not being what it would be reasonable to expect a parent to give him, or that the child is beyond parental control.'* If the child who is abusing has him/herself been abused, and the family circumstances played a major role in that abuse, then it may be relatively straight forward to meet the Section 31 conditions. If this is not the case, then it may be more difficult to use this section of the Act to obtain help for the child. However, Section 31 defines 'harm to a child' to include impairment of emotional, social, and behavioural development. There can be little doubt that abusive behaviour does impair emotional, social and behavioural development. If the home background can be shown i) to have contributed substantially to the abusive behaviour or, ii) not to be conducive to stopping it, then the Section 31 conditions might be said to be satisfied so that a care or supervision order could be imposed. In addition, the Children Act 1989 recognises the need to protect children from future harm. Given that it is indicated that when a child or young person has abused he is likely to continue to abuse without treatment, and if treatment cannot be complied with without an order then it should be possible to satisfy the Section 31 conditions. If Section 31 cannot be interpreted in the ways outlined above, the options under the Children Act seem limited.

4.10 **In the view of the Committee, it is important that authorities interpret the Children Act as indicated above, so that care or supervision orders may be obtained in appropriate cases.**

Criminal Procedures

4.11 Before considering the options available to the court in criminal proceedings, it is important to outline the various options which are open to the police when dealing with a young person who has committed a sexual offence (or any other offence). These are as follows[2]:

4.11.1 To take 'No Further Action' (NFA). This option is invoked with reference to the Attorney General's Guidelines, or when the offence is not regarded as serious enough to warrant prosecution, even though there may be sufficient evidence to prosecute. The informal warning or 'word of advice' is seen as adequate. It is the view of the Committee that this alternative ought not generally to be used where young sexual abusers are concerned.

4.11.2 To 'Caution'. The purpose of a formal caution is to deal quickly and simply with less serious offenders, to divert offenders from the criminal courts, and to reduce chances of re-offending. Home Office guidance suggests that a caution may be administered in the following circumstances:

- where there is sufficient evidence of the young person's guilt to give a realistic chance of conviction, and
- the young person admits that s/he committed the offence, and
- the young person and his/her parents or guardians understand the significance of a caution and give informed consent to it.

If the evidence does not meet the required standard, or if there is no clear or reliable admission of the offence, or if the offence has caused significant harm, then a caution cannot be given. **It is the view of the Committee that a caution on its own is inadvisable, but that such a measure may have a role in combination with a referral to an agency which is able to provide counselling and treatment.** It is recognised, however, that since the treatment will be on a voluntary basis such an arrangement may not always be effective.

4.11.3 To Prosecute. Since 1985, it has been official policy to reduce the use of prosecution for juvenile offenders. It is recognised that by avoiding entrance into the criminal justice system at an early age, a young person's entry into the system can be avoided altogether. The 1990 Home Office Circular states that *'there should be a presumption in favour of not prosecuting juveniles.'* In some circumstances however, prosecution might be the most suitable answer, for example because of the seriousness of the act, or because of the absence of other options.

4.12 Although in certain circumstances young people must be dealt with in the Crown Court (eg, when charged with murder or manslaughter), or in an adult court (eg, when charged jointly with an adult), the Criminal Justice Act 1991 provides that criminal matters involving children from 10-17 years old in England and Wales will be dealt with by magistrates in Youth Courts. Where there is a finding of guilt in these cases there are a number of orders which could enable and encourage treatment to take place:

4.12.1 *Criminal Supervision Order.* Under the Criminal Justice Act 1988, requirements may be attached to supervision orders so that, for example, an offender could be made to take part in a programme of intermediate treatment. The Children Act 1989 also introduces a new power to attach a residence requirement to such an order. The purpose of this requirement is not meant to be punitive, but rather to enable the young person to 'work through' problems whilst living in local authority accommodation. It should be noted that the circumstances in which such a requirement may be imposed are limited. A previous supervision order must have been made with respect to that child and the original order must have imposed a requirement under S 12 (a) (3) CYPA 1969, or alternatively, a residence requirement; the offence must have been committed while that order was in force; the offence must be punishable with imprisonment in the case of a person over 21, and where there is no previous residence requirement, the court must be satisfied that the behaviour which constituted the offence was due, to a significant extent, to the circumstances in which the child was living. (Children Act 1989 Schedule 12 para 23).

4.12.2 *Probation Order.* The Criminal Justice Act 1991 enables probation orders to be made where a person is over the age of 16. A requirement may be added to the order in the interests of securing the rehabilitation of the offender which should enable treatment to be given.

4.12.3 *Custodial Sentence.* At present, the longest custodial sentence which a young person can receive for indecent assault is 12 months detention in a young offender institution, regardless of the number of assaults committed. (Magistrate's Courts Act 1980). Whilst it can be argued that in serious cases this time limitation is inappropriate, real concern exists that any sentence, however long, should be completed without therapeutic intervention. **The Committee believes that it is vital for intensive treatment to be made available to all young sexual abusers who are in custody, and that serious consideration be given to invoking any alternative powers which could ensure that appropriate treatment is made available.**

4.13 Sentencing should take into account what is in the best interests of the child or young person. Some sentences, such as a conditional discharge or a fine would appear to be inappropriate because they would not encourage treatment to take place and may well allow the young person to deny the seriousness of the offence. Societal minimisation of sexual offending, or sexually abusive behaviour ought not to make professionals lose sight of the dangers which are actually involved; nor should the fear of labelling be over-stated. Clearly, an assessment of the abusive behaviour, and the needs of the child or young person must be undertaken prior to sentencing.

4.14 ***The Committee recommends that courts ensure that prior to sentencing, they are provided with an assessment of the young person's background of behaviour, and a list of available facilities, and their suitability for different types of cases. This would allow informed decisions to be taken with regard to disposal.***

4.15 ***The Committee recommends, as a matter of urgency, that the Judicial Studies Board and those responsible for offering training to Magistrates include issues relating to children and young people who abuse other children within their programmes of study.***

The Scottish Context

4.16 When a child or young person under the age of 16 has sexually abused another child, the Social Work (Scotland) Act 1968 provides a system under which compulsory measures of care can be taken to help both the perpetrator and the victim[3]. In Scots law, the age of criminal responsibility is eight; accordingly, when the perpetrator is eight or over, he or she will have committed a criminal offence. The commission of a criminal offence is a ground of referral for compulsory measures of care[4], and if it is thought that the perpetrator requires compulsory measures of care then the reporter takes the case to a children's hearing. If the ground of referral is accepted by the child and the child's parents, the children's hearing can proceed to dispose of the case by ordering the measures of care which are in the child's best interests. If, however, the child and/or parents do not accept the ground of referral, the children's hearing cannot proceed unless the ground of referral is established before the sheriff. Because the reporter is relying on the 'offence' ground, the sheriff must be satisfied beyond reasonable doubt that the perpetrator committed the offence and corroboration remains necessary. If the sheriff makes a finding that the ground is established, then the case is returned to the children's hearing for disposal.

4.17 The child or young person who sexually abuses another child is treated in exactly the same way as a child who commits *any* offence. In other words, the child or young person is seen as being *prima facie* in need of care, not punishment. Therefore the current Scottish system already provides a 'social work/care' framework to deal with this problem. It is only if the ground of referral is denied by the child and/or the parents, that a judicial stage arises and it becomes important that the offence can be proved according to the criminal standard.

4.18 If the sexual abuse was of an extremely serious nature, for example, rape, the case could proceed in the High Court when, on a finding of guilt, the Court has a wide range of orders to deal with the accused, including the power to remit the case to a children's hearing for disposal. When the perpetrator has also been a victim of sexual abuse, a wider range of grounds of referral exist, eg, victim of a Schedule 1 offence, or a member of a household of a person who has committed a Schedule 1 offence.

Chapter 5: Management Issues

Recognising the 'Problem'

5.1 It has taken a long time to persuade society as a whole that children may be sexually abused by parents and other adults; the extent of this type of abuse is still not fully known, and some still choose to deny its existence. To now begin to highlight the fact that the abuser of a child may be another child, an older sibling, school friend, child next door or adolescent babysitter, may be problematic. Some of the difficulties encountered in receiving referrals, and gaining recognition of the level of seriousness of sexually abusive behaviours from young people have already been discussed, and there is evidently a need to overcome varying degrees of denial -from the general public, police services, social services, health services and within the legal system. There appear to be several barriers to recognition:

5.1.1 *People do not want to believe this happens.* We are not, as a society, prepared to think of our children and young people as having sexual awareness, or to think of them as being sexually active. We are even less able to think of them as being sexually abusive. It is easier to look for explanations which fit in with what we can more easily accept about children eg, that they are just 'experimenting' and 'finding out about each other', or with commonly held views based on gender stereotypes eg, 'boys will be boys'. Once such interpretations have been imposed, there is no need to take any further action. There is also the point that professionals in all areas are overburdened and under resourced and could do without new areas of concern.

5.1.2 *Different interpretations will exist of the same incident.* Teachers, for example, who may often be the professionals who first see signs of sexually abusive behaviour patterns may well have had little training in this area and have a narrow view of the interpretations which could be drawn around a certain behaviour. Without some broad-based definitions or guiding criteria, there will inevitably be an inconsistent interpretation of what is going on. People involved with children need an increased knowledge of children's 'normal' behaviour so they have a standard by which to make decisions.

5.1.3 *Fear of labelling* may make certain professionals reluctant to identify a child or young person as an abuser. The dangers of labelling a child or young person as an offender or abuser at an early stage are clear; the child or young person, through the label, may well come to identify with the role, and the abusive aspect of the behaviour could become a permanent feature; the child or young person may be isolated or rejected by his/her family and community, and such labels can have far reaching consequences for the child's or young person's personal relationships and future career.

5.1.4 *Because there are relatively few convictions* in criminal proceedings it is reasonably easy to deny the existence of the 'problem'.

5.2 However, without recognition of the 'problem' it will be hard to advance possible ways of working with it; and so long as society denies there is a problem, abusers will deny it too. Obviously, the development of a clearer, more consistent approach to determining exactly what 'abusive behaviour' is when perpetrated by a child or young person will provide the first step forward in enabling people to recognise and understand what the 'problem' actually is, and will give those in a position to refer the confidence so to do. Some suggested guidelines for identifying abusive behaviour have already been discussed in Chapter 2.8.

5.3 The second factor which has a significant role to play in promoting recognition of the problem, is that of education.

Education

Children

5.4 In the consultative process the importance of openness about sexuality was stressed, particularly in schools. It was felt that such openness should include discussion on relationships and decision-making in relation to sexuality. If children are well informed and empowered, they will be more aware of where to set boundaries, and more assertive; they will be more able to recognise when an act is abusive and aware that it is legitimate for them to say 'no'. Clearly, well planned and relevant sex education for children and young people with learning disabilities is also vital if inappropriate sexual behaviour is to be avoided.

5.5 If such education goes hand in hand with adult awareness raising and education, children and young people will also feel more able and confident to talk to an adult about sexual abuse (either their own abusive behaviour, or their own abuse) without fear of being ignored, chastised, or disbelieved.

5.6 The question was raised throughout the consultative process as to what extent people underestimate the ability of children to understand issues concerning sexuality. A greater, more consistent level of sex education in schools was seen as a positive strategy to begin to change society's current attitudes towards sexuality.

5.7 The Committee also affirm the importance of children and young people in residential care having a programme of preventative education, and an environment which allows for discussion and openness about sexual matters. It is recognised however, that it is hard to develop healthy sexual attitudes in the residential setting, partly owing to the lack of privacy, and partly owing to single sex establishments. In residential care, the atmosphere and attitudes of staff play a crucial educative function, and gender issues such as how the young people are treated and the way relationships between female and male staff are dealt with should not be played down.

5.8 Alongside preventative education packages, health education relating to sexual issues was felt to be important for all children and young people, for example material produced by KIDSCAPE[1].

Adults and Society

5.9 In addition to education in schools, it was felt to be necessary to challenge stereotypes in society which are presented and upheld through, in particular, the media (especially newspapers and magazines and television) and the advertising industry, much of which put forwards a particular view of sexuality. The exposure of children and young people to pornographic material was widely believed to be a significant factor in the development and reinforcement of sexually abusive behaviours in young people. The easy availability of pornographic magazines, pornographic films (on video or via satellite television) and the increased popularity of sexually explicit telephone lines were all implicated throughout the consultations in the development of sexually abusive behaviour patterns in young people.

5.10 Information emerging from clinical work suggests that a consistent 'diet' of pornographic images can be internalised by a child and become part of an overall development of sexually abusive behaviour. For example, pornographic images from films or magazines are used to rehearse fantasies which can eventually be manifested in real behaviours. Young men begin to use telephone lines offering the opportunity to listen to sexually explicit messages. These lines are expensive however, and once addicted to what they offer, a youngster can easily develop a pattern of making obscene telephone calls to members of the general public, using sexually offensive language, which are far cheaper, and perhaps more exciting.

5.11 In addition to these more obvious ways in which children and young people are confronted with sexually explicit material before they may be ready to handle it, more subtle presentations are constantly being made through other media (for a discussion of the use of sexually explicit material in therapy with young sexual abusers see Chapter 3.23.1 - 3.23.2).

5.12 Certain popular tabloid newspapers and television programmes continue to present images of women, both through pictures and the way in which language is used, in ways which serve to maintain the view of women as being 'sex objects'. They promote a particularly negative view of the role of women in society. Men are still portrayed in powerful situations, and are seen as the ones who are 'in control'. Exploitative heterosexual values are upheld as being superior to consensual homosexual ones; the latter frequently being ridiculed and insulted. Advertising campaigns frequently use the image of a child 'dressed up' as an adult, and pressures imposed through the desirable images presented of alcohol and tobacco products encourage young people to feel the need to emulate what they perceive to be typical adult behaviour. All such presentations can be powerful reinforcers to a child or young person who is beginning a path of abusive behaviour.

5.13 A recent report from the Church of England[2] concludes that many children live in a *"prematurely adult"* world of materialism, sex, selfishness, violence and the occult. Toys, magazines, records and clothes aimed at children for commercial reasons leave them *"wallowing in a world of false values"*.

5.14 Adults in general, need to be educated about children's rights and encouraged to confront traditional attitudes which affirm the rights of big over little, strong over weak and men over women. Beginning such educational programmes in school at a young age is one way of introducing this material, but programmes of parental education need to be initiated now, alongside a more informed approach from the media and advertising industries. Society will not, in itself, struggle to develop a definition or understanding of abuse by young people. Parents need to be enabled to take seriously incidents of abuse where the perpetrator is another child or young person. When parents display total disbelief, or when they try to close doors completely and refuse to allow outsider involvement, these attitudes need to be confronted.

5.15 **It is the view of the Committee that there is pressure on children to deal with sexuality before they are ready, and that the increasingly wide availability of pornographic material of all kinds (including telephone sex lines) is a dangerous trend. Work with young perpetrators of sexual abuse suggests that there is a possible link between exposure to pornography and the development of abusive behaviour, and the Committee believes that parents and other carers do have a responsibility to restrict the access of children and young people to this type of material.**

Legitimising the Work

5.16 As already indicated, support for the development of work with young abusers appears to be patchy. Many professionals trying to work in this area do not believe that colleagues and managers feel it is a legitimate area for them to be involved in. Professionals trying to initiate work do not receive referrals because colleagues deny the existence of the problem, and many are undertaking this work in their own time with little or no concession being made in their workload allocation from their managers. In some areas actual opposition from management to the work was reported, with staff being withdrawn because it was not considered part of their workload. Managerial and professional peer group denial of the 'problem' as an area for legitimate professional involvement was certainly raised as a significant hindrance in the development of services; indeed, for reasons stated above, it appears reasonably easy for the existence of the problem to be denied altogether. Similarly, accepting that the problem exists in residential settings is also difficult, as managers fear that establishments will gain negative reputations or that they will attract unfavourable publicity. Some staff who had been interested in running a group work programme for young abusers placed in a residential setting were unable to obtain an adequate number of referrals because of lack of co-operation and trust from other fieldwork colleagues and little support from management.

5.17 This lack of legitimisation of the work with young abusers has meant an absence of agreed guidelines on dealing with the issues, and no established policy on joint working. It has also meant a lack of support, supervision and training for the work. Another point raised was related to the perception that most managerial hierarchies are male dominated. Some claim that part of the denial of the problem from management is a direct result of this gender imbalance. So, education is also an issue for management, in particular the challenging of stereotypical views of male sexuality and male attitudes towards abuse.

5.18 It is the belief of the Committee that the most significant move towards the recognition and legitimisation by agency management, the courts, the police and society as a whole, of work with children and young people who abuse would be the development of an overall system ensuring and enabling multi-agency and multi-disciplinary co-operation in dealing with the problem. Such a system would discourage minimisation and denial and, if adequately resourced, provide a framework within which the referral, assessment and treatment of young people and children who abuse could be efficiently carried out.

Providing a Structure

5.19 The following section looks in more detail at the ways in which an overall structure for working with young abusers might be developed. Throughout the consultative process the need for such a structure was raised, and whilst opinions varied as to the best way to establish this structure, there was little disagreement that a structure is needed. Firstly, such a structure would provide adequate support for staff undertaking the work. It would also provide a consistency of approach in terms of managing individual cases from the point when a child or young person's abusive behaviour initially comes to light, to the point where a decision is taken to intervene and work with the person.

5.20 The Committee recommends that an overall, systematic approach be developed for dealing with cases (alleged or otherwise) where a child or young person has abused another child.

Agency Responsibility

5.21 During the consultative process, much discussion centred around the 'ownership' of the area of work – should responsibility for organisation and management lie with one particular agency which would have the resources to deal with the problem, or should there be shared responsibility, or joint working with one 'lead' agency? Problems were highlighted with the model of 'shared' responsibility; one agency might always hope another would provide the financial and organisational input; good liaison at grass roots level would not necessarily be reflected at points higher up in the structure; one agency might like the power but not be prepared or able to take the financial responsibility.

5.22 Having one 'lead' agency would overcome these problems, and also avoid the problem of other agencies feeling that they did not have a contribution to make. Other problems which could arise as a result of the work being the exclusive territory of one agency or discipline would include the denial of certain skills on offer through other agencies and a narrowing of the philosophical underpinning of the work eg, whether one considers one is working with a 'victim' or an 'offender'. Whatever the model, there needs to be a high degree of co-operation and liaison between disciplines.

5.23 ***The Committee recommends that each agency involved should define its specific responsibility in this area of work, within the context of the overall aims and objectives of the organisation, and should develop a clear statement of agency policy in this matter. This includes Social Services, Police, Probation, Education, and Health.***

5.24 However, the issue of where responsibility ultimately lies is important, not least of all because it will effect the input of resources. Whilst one body of opinion advocates the grounding of this work within the juvenile justice system, the Committee of Enquiry , in complete agreement with the new edition of 'Working Together'[3] views the Child Protection System as the most appropriate to have oversight of work with children and young people who abuse.

5.25 Working Together states that:

"When abuse of a child is alleged to have been carried out by another child or young person, it is important that the appropriate child protection procedures should be followed in respect of both the victim and the alleged abuser.....It is (therefore) an important child protection function to ensure that such behaviour is treated seriously and is always subject to a referral to child protection agencies....Upon receipt of such referral there should be a child protection conference in respect of the alleged abuser..... This should include consideration of possible arrangements for accommodation, education (where applicable) and supervision in the short-term pending the compilation of a comprehensive assessment.....Membership and handling of the conference, including initial plans, should be prescribed in the standard child protection conference. The conference should re-convene following the completion of the comprehensive assessment, to review the plan in the light of the information obtained and to co-ordinate the interventions designed to dissuade the abuser from committing further abusive acts."

5.26 ***The Committee recommends that separate child protection conferences for the victim and the abuser should be organised. This will have major resource implications, especially for Social Service Departments.***

5.27 By locating the work within the Child Protection system rather than the Juvenile Justice system the focus can be widened from dealing with children and young people who have committed a possible offence, to include children and young people who have abused, but are not prosecuted, and children and young people who are involved in inappropriate sexual behaviour. The range of options, including packages of care, is also widened. In addition, if we are to see children and young people who abuse as 'children in need' regardless of their abusive behaviour, and recognise that they will frequently have had a long history of deprivation, this is obviously a more appropriate way of working.

5.28 ***The Committee recommends – in agreement with the Department of Health Guidance – that work with children and young people who sexually abuse other children should take place within the context of Child Protection System. All such work should therefore fall under the auspices of the Area Child Protection Committee (ACPC), whose function it would be to co-ordinate the work, bring it into the child protection conference system, and develop a strategic plan. Directors of Social Services are recommended to ensure that the whole issue of children and young people who abuse other children is put prominently on the agenda.***

5.29 In this system, children and young people would be subject to a child protection conference, and thoroughly assessed (the family would also be assessed). Following on from that, a decision would be made about treatment. The system which exists for abused children and their families could be productively introduced here, whereby a keyworker will be appointed, and a core group works with the child/young person and their family and co-ordinates the assessment and treatment plans. If this work is to be brought into the child protection system, juvenile justice experts, and the Crown Prosecution Service need to be brought into the ACPC system. The ACPC system would need to take into account the interests of the criminal justice system, health service, and child protection system and thought would need to be given as to the best way of including victims (eg, in cases of non-familial abuse) *and* abusers in this inter-agency system.

5.30 Overall, it is believed that such an approach would allow professionals to challenge and confront the young people concerned, at the same time as respecting their individual needs and providing a consistency of approach which does not currently exist. Such a consistent approach would also be beneficial in terms of monitoring and evaluation, providing an overall framework within which information could be gathered on incidence, causation and control of behaviour.

5.31 ***The Committee recommends to all ACPCs that, as part of their annual report, a section should be devoted to the work undertaken with children and young people who sexually abuse other children.***

5.32 The following diagram explains the order of events envisaged by the Committee:

DISCOVERY OR DISCLOSURE OF CHILD OR YOUNG PERSON SEXUALLY ABUSING ANOTHER CHILD

REFERRAL TO POLICE AND/OR SOCIAL SERVICES

INFORMATION SHARING/STRATEGY DISCUSSION
(regarding how the investigation should be handled; probably by telephone, between agency to which referral has been made, and other relevant agencies. Alternatively, a strategy meeting could be called.)

INVESTIGATION/INITIAL ASSESSMENT OF YOUNG PERPETRATOR

INITIAL CHILD PROTECTION CONFERENCE
(to decide if accusation is valid and whether something needs to be taken further. If the case involves an emergency, urgent legal action may be necessary.)

FULL ASSESSMENT

SECOND CHILD PROTECTION CONFERENCE
(to discuss outcome of assessment and possible options for treatment/intervention.)

MANAGEMENT/ INTERVENTION/ TREATMENT

The Role Of the Probation Service

5.33 The probation service currently occupy a crucial role in working with adult sex offenders. Such work is undertaken in the community as well as in penal institutions, and is often shared with other professionals including forensic psychiatrists and psychologists, prison officers and others. In June 1991 a Home Office initiative affecting twenty prisons made therapeutic intervention a requirement for all prisoners convicted of sex offences and serving a sentence of four years or more. Treatment would also be an option for some convicted sex offenders serving less than four years, if they were believed to be dangerous. In addition, the Criminal Justice Act 1991 makes it possible for sex offenders to be supervised after their release on parole up to the full term of their original sentence. Other offenders can only be supervised after release on parole up to the three quarter point of their original sentence (eg, 3 years of a four year sentence).

5.34 Probation Officers have also worked in various settings with young people who have sexually abused. Whilst it has already been stated that work with young perpetrators of sexual abuse should be rooted within the Child Protection System, the experience of the Probation Service in work with adults (as well as with young offenders) should be utilised in the development of services to children and young people who sexually abuse.

5.35 The Committee has been informed by the Home Office Probation Service Division that *"there cannot normally be probation intervention without a mandate, and...... that (there is a commitment) to a policy in that in child protection, as opposed to criminal justice issues, the probation service only becomes involved in private law cases."*

5.36 **The Committee recognises the importance of clarifying the role of the Probation Service in the area of work with young abusers. *In recognition of the level of skills and expertise which already exist within the probation service, the Committee recommends that the Home Office give urgent consideration to ways in which the Probation Service can strengthen their involvement with young abusers.***

Providing a Comprehensive Investigation and Assessment

5.37 The above system for dealing with cases of children and young people who abuse would necessitate the police consulting with social services at an early stage in the investigation. (If investigation has already taken place, then a child protection conference should be considered as soon as the appropriate professionals have the necessary information.) Whilst the current situation means that police could give an instant caution or take a 'No Further Action' (NFA) decision without recourse to Social Services or other agencies, ***the Committee recommends that the police should never NFA a case of this nature nor decide to caution without first contacting, or meeting with social services, and considering the need for a child protection conference to be called. The Home Office should be responsible for drawing such an instruction to the attention of Chief Constables.***

5.38 ***In addition, the Committee recommends to the Police and the Social Service Departments that reports of children or young people having abused other children should be subject to joint investigation.*** It is recognised however, that there are difficulties in arranging joint interviews with the Police and Social Services as part of this process. In child sexual abuse investigations it is the *witness* who is the subject of the joint interview; however, where the investigation involves a young person or child who is suspected of committing the abuse it is the *suspect* who is the subject of the joint interview. In these circumstances, social workers would only normally be involved under the arrangements of PACE (Police and Criminal Evidence Act)[4] where, in the absence of the parent or other adult carer, the social workers' role is to ensure that the young person is interviewed fairly. In the view of the Committee, it would be inappropriate for a social worker to be present at police interviews undertaken under caution, other than in the role described above.

5.39 However, it would be expected that the social worker involved in the joint investigation would be available at the place where the police interview is undertaken, and that the social worker may well be involved in separate interviews with the child. In addition, the social worker must be involved in the planning and initial assessment process with the police. Information sharing between agencies is of great importance and joint decision-making can only take place if all agencies have all the relevant information at their disposal. A copy of the child or young person's statement should therefore be available to the social worker at the earliest opportunity.

5.40 Victim statements are very important in work with sex offenders. They present a more accurate picture of the incident than the worker would be likely to gain from the abuser. (It is important to counteract the abuser's minimisation of the significance of events by having as accurate picture as possible). It is currently very difficult for people working with young perpetrators of sexual abuse (eg, social workers or doctors) to gain access to victim statements. If, however, prior to the collection of a statement, permission was obtained from the victim (or the victim's carer) for statements to be used for specific work with the abuser, it would then be legally possible for victim statements to be made available in such circumstances. The Committee understands the need for restricting access to victim statements particularly when these are recorded on videotape. There is a very real concern that such statements could be used by abusers for their own sexual gratification. This could also endanger victims. However, the need for such statements in the work with the abuser should not be underestimated and, given adequate safeguards, should be possible.

5.41 ***In the light of this, the Committee recommends that the Home Office issue strict guidelines regarding the safe-keeping and restricted use of victim statements (including statements made on video), whilst at the same time ensuring appropriate availability to those bona fide professionals who are undertaking the assessment and/or interventions with the alleged or confirmed perpetrators of sexual abuse.***

5.42 Concern was expressed about the course of action to be taken in the event of a child or young person implicating themselves in abusive behaviour in the course of making a witness statement. Whilst it would be possible, in these circumstances, for the child or young person to be cautioned and the interview continued on the basis of an investigation into the abusive behaviour, the Committee believes this would be wholly inappropriate. If abusive behaviour comes to light in the context of a witness statement, such information should be considered only after the conclusion of the interview; consultation between agencies should take place prior to an investigation into the abusive behaviour being undertaken.

5.43 Decisions about the 'disposal' of a case should not just depend upon the investigation. Implicit within the need for a structured approach to dealing with cases of children and young people who abuse is the need for a skilled and detailed full assessment to take place. Such an assessment should be undertaken at an early stage in the process, with a multi-agency, multi-disciplinary approach, with information being gathered from health, education, police, social services, family and other relevant sources; the skills of a wide range of professionals can appropriately be used in this context. The assessment of children and young people who abuse needs to be seen as a specialism, and would benefit from a nationally agreed protocol.

5.44 The Committee believes that any assessment process should take the following factors, amongst others, into account:

- The individual should be seen as a whole person, as a social individual. Abusive behaviour should not be looked at in isolation from more positive aspects and strengths.
- The nature of the incident(s). Chapter 2.8 has described some basic guidelines for considering whether or not a behaviour is sexually abusive.
- Whether or not responsibility has been accepted for the incident.
- The level of risk or dangerousness that a young person poses to others as well as to him/herself.
- Patterns of behaviour and the young person's understanding of that behaviour. What is the extent of the child/young person's sexual development? Has there been use of, or contact with pornographic material?
- Family background and support. This is important in terms of determining the family's commitment to care for the child or young person and the extent of their belief that abuse has taken place. It is also necessary to consider relationships within the family, whether or not there has been abuse in the family, and if so between whom, the extent of social relationships (including school), and the ethnic and cultural background of the family.
- Options for placement and treatment. The assessment should establish a relevant package of care for the young person, which could include referral to a court, or other appropriate action.

Provision of Services

5.45 Any efficient assessment service will only function if it is backed up by appropriate treatment or behaviour management programmes ie, if there is a range of service provision available to meet the particular needs of each individual. The

Committee of Enquiry is agreed that there needs to be a 'continuum' of different services for different groups of young abusers. Abusive behaviour ranges from sexually motivated murder and teenage rape including the use of violence and weapons to inappropriate sexual behaviour by younger children, or young people with learning disabilities. Young people who are abusing large numbers of other children with violence have very different needs from children who have engaged in sexually inappropriate behaviour with one or two other children and have not used violence or coercion in their behaviour. There is also the need to take into account whether or not the child or young person is known to have been abused themselves. Resources need to be available for children and young people at both ends of the spectrum, and at various points in between.

5.46 Whilst assessment will aim to determine the appropriate course of intervention to be taken with a child or young person who has abused, this will only be of use if a range of treatment options are available. Non-intervention may allow an adolescent to develop a deviant sexual identity, and inappropriate intervention can have an equally negative impact. In the consultative process it became evident that some young abusers are being inappropriately placed; dangerous youngsters, for example, being held in open conditions with inadequate supervision such that they have had the opportunity to continue their abusive behaviour against other children. Similarly, other youngsters have been held inappropriately in secure conditions with no clear strategy, treatment or management plan.

5.47 ***The Committee recommends to all agencies involved, the idea of a 'continuum of care'. Such a system would make available – on either a legally mandated or voluntary basis – different services ranging from child guidance clinics (who will be in a position to work with children displaying pre-abusive behaviours) to secure accommodation offering treatment programmes. The continuum would also include community based treatment programmes with accommodation, community based programmes with the child or young person living at home, or with foster parents, or programmes where the family is enabled to provide support for the young person living in the home.***

5.48 Whilst most children or young people who have learning disabilities will not act in a sexually inappropriate or abusive way, problems of this nature may arise. Consequently, attention needs to be paid to the development of appropriate ways of working with children or young people with learning disabilities who have developed this type of behaviour. The Committee is aware of one programme for adults with learning disabilities in the USA[5], and the authors of this programme are confident that quality treatment programming can be of benefit to this group of people and to the community at large. Given this experience, the Committee believes that attention should be paid in the development of a 'continuum of care' to the inclusion of treatment programmes which are suitable for those young people with learning disabilities who are involved in sexually abusive, or sexually inappropriate behaviour.

5.49 The development of a system involving a 'continuum of care' may well mean that some services would need to be developed on a regional basis, with others more locally based.

5.50 ***The Committee recommends that in order to create a 'continuum of care', and to address the need for management and intervention, a network of specific specialist services should be established throughout the UK. The Committee recommends that the Department of Health and the Home Office act as 'brokers', facilitating the development of projects and funding the shortfall incurred in the initial opening period. Such projects could well be managed by local authorities or voluntary organisations, as well as health authorities, or the probation service.***

5.51 This network of facilities will need to develop through a strengthening of existing services and the creation of new provision.

5.52 ***The Committee recommends that all agencies establishing projects should require those projects to have a specified programme which identifies the problems to be addressed and the methods to be used, the time scale, the aims and objectives, and the proposed method of evaluation.***

The Role of Residential Care in the Continuum of Care

5.53 The difficulties and issues arising out of the placement of children and young people who abuse within a residential setting have already been discussed (see Chapter 3.38-3.43). If a 'continuum of care' is to be developed however, there will inevitably be a need for certain services to offer a residential component, and residential provision does allow for a more intensive form of work (either with individuals, or groups), if this is what is deemed necessary.

5.54 **The Committee believes that there is a need within the Continuum of Care for the establishment of more specialist residential treatment facilities for children and young people who have abused other children, who are assessed as being in need of this type of intervention.**

5.55 It is acknowledged that such facilities are costly because they require all care staff to be fully trained and supported by, for example, psychologists and/or psychiatrists. Even though such facilities will undoubtedly serve more than one local authority, no system currently exists to facilitate their establishment. It is in the early period of the development of projects that costs are especially high. Staff need to be in post before clients are actually accepted into the project, and it takes time for a project to establish its reputation and become fully used.

5.56 Where residential establishments are to take children or young people who have abused, it is crucial that appropriately trained staff are placed there, and that they are well supervised and supported in their work (see Chapter 6). It is vital to ensure an appropriate gender balance in the staffing ratio, bearing in mind that issues of sexuality and gender are at the forefront in this type of work. Certainly, children or young people known to have abused, should never be placed in a residential setting where their abusive behaviour will not be addressed, managed or worked with in any way. If a young person needs to develop a 'cover story' to hide their abusive behaviour (either for their own protection, or to prevent a difficult situation arising) then the Committee would like to suggest that the placement is an inappropriate one. The development of 'cover stories' can be seen as a denial of the rights of other non-abusing young people in the same establishment. Habitual denial and lying about a child's problems may avoid immediate stress and discomfort, but without doubt makes appropriate assessment and intervention progressively more difficult, even impossible. Cover stories maintained by a young person whilst in residential care may subsequently be incorporated in the lies and cognitive distortions which are characteristic of adult offenders.

5.57 Although it is possible to recommend that abused children and abusing children should not be placed together, the Committee recognises that this may in practice, be impossible. In his recent report on residential childcare, Sir William Utting (1991)[6] recommends that abused children, and abusing children should not be accommodated in the same establishment (implicitly suggesting that abusing children should be placed in more specialist facilities). Although, in theory, this may be a desirable objective, the Committee has already stated the difficulties of definition because of the existence of a continuum between inappropriate sexual behaviour and 'clear cut' abuse. Further, a good number of children who sexually abuse have themselves been abused, and unless one makes the criteria for accommodation rather more sophisticated, this may lead to conflict and uncertainty rather than assisting the situation.

5.58 For example, it will not always be known upon placement if a child or young person has a history of abuse and/or abusive behaviour; it is not possible to accurately predict future behaviour at the time of placement. However, if a child begins to display sexually abusive behaviour towards others, or it is discovered that the child has been abused or involved in abusive behaviour, it may not always be appropriate or desirable to immediately seek to move the child to a different establishment. A practice example may help to illustrate this point. A fifteen year old girl was systematically sexually abused in her foster placement over a number of years. She did not disclose immediately, but behaved in such a way that she was removed from the placement and placed in a residential community home. There she disclosed her abuse, and this was confirmed by the abuser. During her stay in residential care she sexually abused two younger males, but did not believe she had done anything wrong because full sexual intercourse had not taken place. Would this young woman, or indeed the two younger boys, be helped by her summary removal from the placement, or would appropriate therapeutic intervention and increased staff supervision be a more suitable way of handling the situation?

5.59 An additional complication involved in trying to separate abused and abusing youngsters in residential care is the fact that sexual abuse always takes place in an atmosphere of secrecy, and staff may well be unaware that it is happening. Furthermore, there may be advantages which can be gained from dispersing children and young people with residential needs amongst a number of settings, rather than creating one focused setting for those who have been involved in abusive behaviour. The simple statement that sexually abusing children or young people should not be placed with victims of sexual abuse is seen by the Committee as a simplistic one, which denies the complexity of the issue.

5.60 Whenever young people are placed together (whether or not they have been involved in abusing behaviour) issues concerning sexuality are bound to be raised. The Committee believes that such issues need to be dealt with in an atmosphere of complete openness, allowing the young people and staff to explore issues together in an honest and frank, yet protective environment. This could take place through detailed sex education, education about social and sexual relationships, and the provision of normative role models. The latter means that staff need to be clear about setting their own sexual boundaries, and be able to present positive models of social relationships which include respect for each individual. They also need to ensure that gender issues are addressed by presenting non-sexist behaviours and ideas. Staff need to be vigilant about the possibility of abuse, and children and young people should be encouraged to speak openly about issues like sexual harassment or physical intimidation.

5.61 It is important that children and young people are treated with respect and have a voice in the every day living environment. As in all situations, young people need to be affirmed as valued individuals who are able to express their opinion in the full knowledge that it will be listened to and heard. In this regard, the residential setting can provide a good opportunity to empower young people, and assertiveness training can be a very productive way of beginning to achieve these goals.

5.62 The Committee also stresses the importance of the development of effective complaints procedures for children and young people living in residential care, as stated in the Children Act 1989. Access to a telephone which can be used in privacy, and information about how to reach helplines or independent advocates such as ChildLine, NCH Carelines and the Advocacy Scheme for Children will support children in reaching help if abuse is occurring in their care situation. ***The Committee recommends that all agencies should ensure that in residential settings for children and young people such facilities and information are made available in order to enable children or young people to feel more able to report incidences of abuse perpetrated against them, either by other children or staff.***

5.63 ***The Committee recommends to all Social Service Departments and Voluntary Child Care agencies that decisions regarding the placement of children in residential care should be made on an individual basis, taking into account the nature of the abusive behaviour, the vulnerability of the children or young people living in the establishment, the level of training which the staff have received, the ethos of the establishment, and the resource implications of such a placement. In making decisions about a placement however, the needs of the child or young person who has been involved in abusive behaviour should not take priority over the needs of the other children and young people in the establishment.***

5.64 There is unquestionably a demand for therapeutic, secure, specialised residential provision for those young sexual abusers whose assessment indicates the need for a higher level of security. Currently, such abusers could be placed in Youth Treatment Centres (of which there are two in England), secure hospitals for those suffering from a psychiatric illness, Young Offenders Institutions, or the Aycliffe

Centre for Children. A recently announced initiative from the Home Secretary aims to ensure that sex offenders who have received a minimum sentence of four years should be able to receive treatment. This may include young sex offenders sentenced to a period of youth custody. Whether, given the length of sentence limitation, such a provision will allow many young sex offenders to be treated remains to be seen.

5.65 ***The Committee recommends to the Home Office and the Department of Health, that intensive treatment be made available to all young sexual abusers who are in custody. If the Home Office Initiative mentioned above does not ensure that all young sex offenders sentenced to a period of youth custody receive some form of intensive intervention which is focused on their sexually abusive behaviour, then resources must be made available to ensure that such intervention is introduced.***

The Role of Foster Care in the Continuum of Care

5.66 Children or young people who abuse may well be in need of a foster placement. The family environment and parenting which such a placement can offer will be likely to fulfil many of the needs of the young abuser, and such a placement must only be made following an assessment of those needs. A foster placement must also only be made as part of an overall treatment/intervention plan which includes specialist resources for the child and intensive support and specialist advice for the foster carers. ***The Committee recommends that such placements should never be made if there are younger, or developmentally less advanced children or young people in the foster placement.***

5.67 Foster carers taking on such a placement must have received specialist training in this area of work, and they need to be enabled to deal in an honest and open way with issues of sexuality and sexual behaviour.

5.68 Arrangements for the placement should pay attention to sleeping arrangements, open door policies (ie, no closed bedroom doors with an emphasis on privacy), and self-protection training (such as that produced by KIDSCAPE[7], for example) for all children in the placement. Serious consideration must be given to the protection of other children in the same placement, whether these children are the natural children of the foster carers, or other foster children. Where it is known that a child or young person about to be placed has exhibited sexually abusive behaviour, the Committee recommends that the placing agency must always fully inform the foster carers of the circumstances.

5.69 The level of contact with professionals will need to be high in the initial stages of the placement and foster carers must have easy access to relevant professionals when needed. Foster carers need to be clear about their own sexual boundaries and be able to present positive models of social relationships, which include respect for each individual. They also need to ensure that gender issues are addressed, presenting non-sexist behaviours and ideas. Foster carers would need to be able to talk openly with professionals about their own sexuality and relationships. They would need to be vigilant to the possibility of abuse and be able to speak openly about issues such as sexual harassment or physical intimidation.

5.70 Where children or young people are continuing to live in the community with foster carers (or parents) while receiving treatment, there is a need to ensure that treatment received outside the residential environment is supported and continued within that setting. This demands that those undertaking the treatment ensure that carers are informed of what is being done and how they can support the process.

The Role of the School in the Continuum of Care

5.71 As indicated elsewhere in the report, the role of education in preventing the development of sexually abusive attitudes and behaviour cannot be underestimated (see chapter 5.4 - 5.15). More specifically, schools have a significant role to play in recognising abusive behaviour when it occurs and in taking appropriate action, and also in supporting any child or young person who has been involved in sexually abusive behaviour and is involved in a programme of intervention.

5.72 ***The Committee recommends that where it has been established that a child or young person has been involved in sexually abusive behaviour, the school must be informed.*** If the recommendation of the Committee (see Chapter 5.28), and the guidance in 'Working Together'[8] are followed, then a child protection conference will be held in which representatives of the school would have an important contribution to make.

5.73 Teachers, as significant adults in the life of the child or young person, must offer practical and emotional support to any child or young person who is involved in a programme of treatment aimed at addressing abusive behaviour patterns. They must be encouraged to feed back any relevant information regarding the behaviour of the child or young person to those other professionals who are more directly involved in the treatment programme. ***The Committee recommends that the teacher who is normally responsible for liaison with the child protection agencies is the most appropriate person to oversee any involvement with a child or young person who has sexually abused.***

Collecting Information

5.74 ***The Committee recommends to the Department of Health that a national information service should be established, which would receive details of all projects working with young sex abusers, for the benefit of professionals, courts and carers/parents etc. The Committee believes that there are various options for the organisation of such a network, but suggests the following model as one potential way forward:***

5.74.1 ***Each project working with young sex abusers should be required to notify the local ACPC of the existence of the service, and the nature of the services provided. ACPCs could then maintain an annually reviewed list of provisions for children and young people who have abused other children. On an annual basis, these lists could be forwarded to the Department of Health, who would have responsibility for compiling an annually updated register of such provision. The DoH would be responsible for disseminating this information.***

Practice Guidelines

5.75 In the view of the Committee it is vital that guidelines for good practice should be established. These guidelines should:

- be multi-disciplinary and therefore apply to any professional embarking on an intervention with a child or young person who has sexually abused;
- ensure that a full assessment is undertaken in each case, on the basis of which decisions could be made regarding treatment, or other appropriate interventions;
- set standards, within the limitations of present knowledge, for the content of assessment and the nature of intervention, as well as its appropriateness in certain circumstances;
- recommend the levels of knowledge, experience and consultation needed in order to undertake various activities;
- establish ethical guidelines with respect to this work;
- give guidance for appropriate networking with all relevant agencies.

5.76 Such guidance would need to be endorsed by all relevant disciplines, making it acceptable across disciplinary boundaries.

5.77 ***The Committee recommends that Government departments (Department of Health, Home Office, Department of Education and Science, Lord Chancellor's Department) be responsible for developing and disseminating***

nationally agreed guidelines, ensuring input from Area Child Protection Committees. Alternatively, the Government could commission a national organisation such as NOTA[9] to do this on its behalf. It is most appropriate that these guidelines emerge from, and are endorsed by, a multi-disciplinary organisation recognised nationally, and with as large a membership as possible.

Scotland

5.78 The Committee acknowledges that the above recommendations for structuring the work with children and young people who abuse are not directly transferable to the situation in Scotland. From the consultation in Scotland, the Committee is aware that the thinking in relation to the work task is no different and that the major theoretical and practical issues described in the report are valid for Scotland. The legal differences are described elsewhere in the report (see Chapter 4.16 - 4.18), and organisationally, there are also clear differences.

5.79 The role of the Reporter, for example, seems to be crucial in the Scottish context[10]. The Reporter's role in considering whether a children's hearing should be arranged and in making initial investigations into the circumstances makes it vital that all agencies involved, when they are aware of a situation in which a child or young person is, or may be, involved in sexually abusive behaviour, ensure the Reporter is informed. This should be done prior to making a decision about disposal of the case by the investigative agencies unless immediate action to protect the public or the child or young person is deemed necessary. It would be the role of the Reporter to decide what actions to take next, no doubt in consultation with the relevant agencies and the Procurator Fiscal where indicated. Although the Reporter has a pivotal role, this should not mean that the agencies involved in this work (such as the Social Work Departments, Police, Health Services, Education, Procurator Fiscal) are not in a position to ensure that systems are in place to deal with the issues involved in working with children/ young people who sexually abuse.

5.80 The Area Review Committees should, in this context, take a leading role in developing policies and procedures for handling such cases, (as with the ACPCs in England and Wales), and for encouraging the development of appropriate treatment/intervention facilities. In this context, the need for this kind of work has already been acknowledged in the Scottish Office publication, Effective Intervention: Child Abuse Guidance on Co-operation in Scotland 1989[11], which draws attention to the need for specialist programmes for Child Sexual Abuse perpetrators, stating,

"Properly directed programmes of behaviour modification or retraining could do much to contain a growing social problem, reducing the pressures on children and ultimately helping to deploy resources more effectively" (see paras 5.18 to 5.22 in 'Effective Intervention'.)

5.81 The guidance in the same publication under 4.37 states,

"Where the abuse is alleged to have been perpetrated by a person who is a child, whether known to the abused child or not, it is important that the Social Work Department and the Reporter be involved at the outset to provide the necessary support and assess the need for compulsory measures of care".

5.82 The Committee strongly commends this statement as it would allow for further development of Projects working with young people/children who sexually abuse within a system which can give full attention both to the welfare needs of the child/ young person and to the offending aspect of their behaviour.

5.83 The Committee is aware that the 1989 publication is to be redrafted and reissued and is also aware that there is a current review of the Child Care Law in Scotland. The Committee expresses the hope and expectation that the issue of children/ young people who abuse will be given attention and that the recommendations made in this report will be of help in this process.

Chapter 6: Training and Supervision

Training

6.1 Throughout the consultative process, a general dissatisfaction was expressed with the current level of training available for those working with children or young people who have abused other children. Indeed, there appears to be little, or no specific formal training available for staff or foster carers who are working, or seeking to work in this field. The particular problems of untrained staff working in residential settings have already been alluded to. A large amount of the 'training' currently experienced by staff working in this area has come from informal meetings with others doing similar work, and through sharing experiences, working methods and associated problems. Staff with a small amount of (possibly self-developed) expertise in the field are being expected to train and support others.

6.2 ***The Committee sees training as being vital for ALL those working with children and young people who sexually abuse other children. It is recommended that this training be aimed at:***

- ***Primary carers (foster carers, residential workers). Often this group tend to be overlooked for training purposes, and training is not seen as a crucial, integral part of the role they play;***
- ***Specialist Practitioners (including child protection liaison teachers);***
- ***Supervisors;***
- ***Senior Management;***
- ***Members of all ACPCs.***

6.3 The Committee does not believe that it is necessarily effective to train a few senior people and hope that the knowledge will 'trickle down' to others. A more formalised and structured approach to training is required, which begins with basic awareness training as part of the general education of social workers, psychologists, psychiatrists, and other relevant professionals. Whilst this training should enable staff to recognise that they have skills and experience learnt elsewhere which they can bring to their work with young abusers, more specific areas need to be systematically covered.

6.4 ***The Committee of Enquiry recommends that proposals should be drawn up for various levels of training, and suggests that training should aim to encompass the following areas:***

- ***An examination of attitudes to abuse and sexuality;***
- ***The general physical, emotional and sexual development of children;***
- ***The nature of abusive behaviour and definitions;***
- ***The development of skills needed to work with young abusers;***
- ***An overview of existing theory and practice in the field, in recognition that no one theory has the ultimate answer in this work;***
- ***General experience in working therapeutically with young people;***
- ***An overview of what can and cannot be achieved through particular therapeutic stances;***
- ***How to undertake assessments, particularly with regard to risk and future dangerousness;***
- ***An understanding of the psycho-sexual socialisation of adults, which can lead to attitudes which may be exploited or exploitative - from sociological, feminist and family systems perspectives;***

- ***The development of skills needed to work in consultation with other professionals;***
- ***Supervised Practice;***
- ***Work with people with learning disabilities who display sexually inappropriate behaviour;***
- ***Work with female sex offenders.***

6.5 Clearly many of the components mentioned above, whilst crucial for those practitioners working with young abusers, are not uniquely relevant to them. The Committee believes that training for work with abusers can, to a certain extent, go 'hand in hand' with training for work with abused children. Basic and more advanced child abuse courses should certainly include teaching about work with young sexual abusers. *High level, specialised training,* however, must also be available, for those with an intensive, high degree of involvement with this work, and for those who are supervising workers in this area.

6.6 ***The Committee recommends that ACPCs and their constituent agencies encourage the development of training in this area of work and ensure that appropriate levels of training are available to all staff working with children and young people who sexually abuse other children. In order to facilitate this, each agency should appoint a lead officer to take responsibility for the development of comprehensive training programmes for staff. The Committee further recommends that CCETSW, the Royal College of Psychiatrists, the British Psychological Society and other training institutions offer and/or specify relevant training for those people likely to encounter or offer a service to young sexual abusers in the course of their professional duties.***

6.7 Whilst such formal training is of paramount importance, the Committee acknowledges the importance of more informal training to be gained through 'sharing days' which can be helpful, especially with regard to enabling staff to come to terms with the realities of practice. Workers are conscious of the lack of guidelines and relevant research, and have traditionally relied on each other for support and exchange of information. Although the Committee of Enquiry would not wish to see this as a substitute for formal training and supervision, it would wish to emphasize the value of national conferences, debates in journals, and other sources of written, disseminated information from people working in the field.

6.8 **The Committee acknowledges that it will take a long time to develop adequate levels of training in this area of work. It will be even longer before the impact of that training is felt at practice level. However, there is an urgent need to develop services at the present time, and this cannot wait until adequate training is established. Current service development needs to take place in the context of the limited experience which is available. The implementation of a process of training as outlined above in 6.6 should however ensure that the growth of services for young abusers, the increasing experience of workers, and the enrichment of the existing knowledge base can all take place in parallel.**

Supervision and Support

6.9 Working in any area of sexual abuse brings with it a series of difficulties which need to be acknowledged. The added complication of facing childhood sexualisation and inappropriate sexual behaviour in young people makes the work emotionally pressurised. Add to this, the high level of denial experienced in society at large, the lack of legitimacy given to the work, and the paucity of resources to give additional help, it is clear that in order to bring skilled intervention to children, a comprehensive system of support and supervision is needed for staff.

6.10 Uncertainties about the legitimacy of the work, and the complex consequences of denial combine to create a great pressure on the member of staff. Denial is an enormously debilitating factor to staff who are attempting to work with these children and they can experience a whole range of reactions, from being ignored to actual hostility from other professionals. Managerial denial of the need to work with young abusers can leave staff exposed and isolated, and unclear as to whether or not this is a legitimate area in which they should be working. They can easily be made to feel like 'scapegoats'. A member of staff may see the need to work with a particular youngster who has been involved in abusive behaviour, yet if colleagues and managers are denying the value of professional involvement in this area, or are claiming that it should be the responsibility of another agency, then the member of staff will inevitably experience a conflict of interests.

6.11 Supervision and support in this area of work are important for several reasons.

6.11.1 Work of this nature can evoke intense emotions, create mixed feelings for workers about their own childhood sexuality, and cause confusion about what is 'normal' sexual development and what is abuse.

6.11.2 Some staff may well have been abused themselves as children and will need to recognise and deal with this experience. As most models of intervention with abusers require the worker to confront the abuser, he or she may feel more vulnerable in the process.

6.11.3 Experience and insight are essential in work with abusers of any age. The staff member must be able to conceptualise the problem as well as understand the emotional impact of the work. Good supervision is of paramount importance in this process.

6.11.4 Recognising these elements in working with children or young people who have sexually abused, workers may conclude that it is not appropriate for them to be working in this area. This will need to be discussed with a supervisor. It needs to be recognised that it will require a great deal of confidence for a worker to acknowledge, 'it is not right for me to be doing this work.' Sensitive supervision, with clear and understood boundaries between the personal and professional material being exposed, can enable staff to give thorough consideration to the impact which the work is having upon them, and to come to the right decisions about how this is going to be handled. Inability to undertake this kind of work should not be seen as failure on the part of the worker.

6.12 In the course of the consultations, it became evident that many staff currently involved in work with young abusers feel completely unsupported, and are denied the benefits which well-organised, structured and frequent supervision can bring. Sometimes supervisors seem to be unaware of the difficulties faced by staff who are working in isolation; it has been known for managers to use words like, "Oh, so you can't handle it yourself then?", when a member of staff requests support!

6.13 The following factors appear to be significant in preventing adequate supervision from happening:

6.13.1 As a relatively 'new' area of work, many people in positions of supervisory responsibility do not have the relevant experience to enable them to support their staff who have become involved in working with young abusers. Any supervision which does take place can very easily become focused purely on case management. Whilst the importance of case management as one part of the supervisory process is acknowledged, the aspect of the process which should be about enabling the member of staff to do the job can be neglected.

6.13.2 There appears to be a tendency for supervisors to believe that the more experienced a member of staff gets in the area, the less need there is for supervision. However, as has been suggested above, there is a need for even the most experienced worker to 'unload' this material from time to time, to enable them to maintain a clear perspective in planning future work with children and families.

6.13.3 Supervisors need to be emotionally prepared to handle the material, and able to use appropriate language with their staff. Supervisors who have not adequately confronted aspects of their own sexuality, or who feel uncomfortable discussing matters related to work with young abusers will be unable to offer good support and supervision to other staff.

6.14 At the heart of any organisational response to staff working with children and young people who abuse other children is the attitude of management to the importance of the work. If managers continue to deny the need for any constructive input with young abusers it will be difficult for reliable and suitable supervisory arrangements to be established for those staff who take this work on board. An agency or organisation needs to enable supervision to take place. Crucial to this is the way in which arrangements and resources are made available for training supervisors. Any organisation involved in work with young abusers needs to undertake a comprehensive audit of skills held by those members of staff involved in, or potentially involved in the work. A commitment needs to be given to provide training where necessary; both for 'frontline' workers, and for supervisors. Those supervisors with skills should be encouraged to share those skills and to get involved in the development of other supervisors and managers.

6.15 It may be necessary to involve outside consultants from time to time to cover more specific aspects of the work. The issue of using consultants who are not directly employed by the same agency as the staff member does raise questions around ensuring standards and confidentiality, and whether or not the consultant would be expected to inform the employing agency if the practitioner's work is unacceptable. Agencies will need to think through these considerations before taking on board any consultancy.

6.16 Regarding the difficulties experienced in working in isolation, the structure of the agency also needs to allow for the possibility of joint working. Opportunities also need to be afforded for group supervision, to enable staff to express feelings and anxieties in a context where others will have had similar experiences. Adequate time needs to be provided in work programmes for regular supervisory sessions; these should be seen as a crucial component of the work, not as an optional extra.

6.17 Many areas of work with abusers leave the worker vulnerable, and possibly open to disciplinary proceeding if they are not working within clearly agreed parameters. A further factor then, which could assist staff in doing the work, and which would make them feel more confident and supported in the work, would be the existence of practice and ethical guidelines. The development of such guidelines is discussed in more detail in Chapter 5.75 - 5.77.

6.18 Whilst all the above issues are relevant for those staff working in residential care, and foster carers, there are some specific concerns. Staff working in residential establishments and foster carers are particularly vulnerable as far as support and supervision are concerned. They are the 'front line' workers in managing a young abuser in a situation where both the young abuser and other residents may be at risk. They may also be less likely to have received any specialist training, and may not even be aware of the nature of the offences or behaviours of the young person. Gender issues are particularly important in residential care and staff groups need support and training in trying to maximise their ability to protect themselves and others.

6.19 ***Overall, with regard to support and supervision, the Committee makes the following recommendations to those agencies undertaking work, or seeking to undertake work with young sexual abusers:***

- ***Managers must recognise, as a matter of urgency, the need for the skilled supervision of staff who are doing this work.***
- ***Supervision should be regular and take place regardless of the level of experience of the workers.***
- ***In addition to personal supervision, recognition should be given to organised staff groups within which workers from different disciplines can increase their level of skill and understanding whilst having the opportunity to work through their feelings and anxieties.***
- ***A thorough audit of skills held by those involved in supervising this work should be conducted, and training provided where there is a deficit. This may entail a need for external consultancy, and this should be made available where necessary.***

Chapter 7: Research Issues

7.1 The urgent need to take seriously the problem of children and young people who sexually abuse other children has already been fully discussed. However, the immediate need to develop a more comprehensive system of working with young abusers should not negate the need for reflective and fully evaluated management and intervention programmes. In conjunction with systematic attempts to manage the difficulties presented by children and young people who abuse other children, efforts must also be made to increase understanding of the nature of the problem, its evolution and the impact of management and intervention strategies. This calls for the development of an extensive and wide-ranging programme of research.

The Nature and Evolution of the Problem

7.2 Much has been learned about adult sexual offenders and their behaviour. In recent years, considerable progress has been made in their systematic assessment and in attempting to modify their offending behaviour. Such work has resulted in speculation about the factors involved in the evolution of sexually abusive behaviour, to such an extent that it is possible to identify some factors which must be the focus of the efforts of researchers and other professionals working with children and young people (see Chapter 3.45-3.62).

7.3 Theoretically at least, it is possible for a child's development to follow several paths with respect to being abused and displaying abusive behaviour. Children who have been sexually abused and those who have not, may or may not themselves subsequently behave in a sexually abusive manner. Of course, many other factors must also be studied with respect to the development of sexually abusive behaviour, and the potential impact of such factors on subsequent behaviour may be similarly represented. When attempting to evaluate the relationship between a child having been sexually abused and becoming a child perpetrator of abuse, additional factors must be measured and analysed. These factors would include:

- circumstances preceding the abuse,
- the nature of the abusive experience(s),
- circumstances and experiences following abuse,
- characteristics of the child victim.

7.4 The nature of any of the above variables may predispose the child to becoming an abuser (and perhaps ultimately an adult offender), or mitigate against such an outcome. It is accepted that the occurrence of a precocious sexual experience, including abuse, is not, in itself, sufficient to cause a child to become a perpetrator; not least because current experience suggests that most victims are female and most perpetrators male. Furthermore, there is some evidence to suggest that boys and girls respond differently to being abused, and this may give a clue to the apparently greater risk of male victims becoming perpetrators. Thus gender (and its physiological, social and psychological correlates) must constitute a major variable in research. It is not only a factor in its own right, but also a determinant of the nature and experience of other factors, such as the process of being abused and the ability to cope with that abuse on a long-term basis.

7.5 All factors and their interrelationships must be researched, described and understood from a perspective which is fully informed by child development, both physical and psychological[1]. This is particularly the case for young children who begin to engage in sexually abusive behaviour, because their emotional, cognitive and social faculties are qualitatively so different from those of older children, or adults. Furthermore, it is also probable that the onset and impact of adolescence constitutes one of the major factors determining behaviour in early, if not later, adulthood. Therefore, the existing body of knowledge relating to child and adolescent development is likely to have much to offer to any study which attempts to understand children and young people who have or may have been involved in sexually abusing other children.

Impact of Management Strategies

7.6 O'Hagan (1989)[2] has reviewed the research on child sexual abuse and makes an observation which is also specifically applicable to the issue of children and young people who sexually abuse other children. He laments the dearth of what he regards as the most significant type of research of all ...

".....namely, how agencies like social services, police and the judiciary respond to the abuse. There is ample evidence available for researchers now to demonstrate how influential this variable is. Apart from the intrinsic merit of researching it, the research would be most welcome to individual professionals, and to training establishments."

7.7 Research into how agencies respond to children and young people who are believed to have abused other children would need to cover a considerable range of research foci, including how cases are actually dealt with by families, professionals and the legal system and the outcomes of specific treatment/ management approaches.

7.8 In all cases, such research will only be successful if the complexity of agencies which presently deal with allegations of abuse perpetrated by children or young people are committed to research as a priority. This is particularly so with respect to research undertaken during the period in which an allegation is investigated, when the collection of data coincides with the forensic process of gathering evidence. Considerable care must be taken either to ensure that the two processes are quite distinct or to make explicit the degree of overlap between them.

Difficulties Researching Children and Young People who Abuse Other Children

7.9 In common with other areas in which childhood experiences may or may not express themselves in a particular manner in adulthood, it is some years from the commencement of research that clear evidence is accumulated with respect to an overall developmental perspective. Thorough longitudinal studies therefore need to be commenced as soon as possible.

7.10 Although the total numbers of children who sexually abuse other children are significant, for the purposes of research, these would need to be sub-categorised according to age, gender, and the nature of the act(s). Other factors may also be of significance, such as cultural background, cognitive development etc. The necessity for such sub-categorisations can result in small sample sizes; this can be problematic in terms of making inferences about other populations. A partial solution to this problem would be the development of standardised assessment measures. Alongside a system of liaison between researchers at a national level, this would allow data from several settings to be comparable, and datasets to be integrated in order to produce more valid and generalisable results.

7.11 Children who have sexually abused are often subjected to significant interventions in their lives. It is difficult to design research which discriminates between the effects of an experience or behaviour and the effects of the responses of other people to that experience or behaviour. The latter, whilst having a significant impact upon the child, will also to a large extent be contingent upon the behaviour itself.

7.12 In order for research results to be valid, it is most desirable that adequate controls are established. Research would be welcomed which compared children who have sexually abused with *matched* controls of non-abusing children and children who have engaged in non-sexually abusive behaviour (both boys and girls). Unfortunately, there are serious ethical problems facing researchers wishing to gather data relating to sexual interest and behaviour in children and adolescents as control subjects. Information which could reasonably be requested from a child who has engaged in sexually abusive behaviour could not necessarily be requested from a child who has not engaged in such behaviour. The information is highly personal and any attempt to elicit it would be likely to be considered unacceptable or even abusive in itself. Research which has attempted to gather normative data on sexuality in children has been undertaken[3], and has produced some useful results. However, practical problems are often reported by researchers in this area. For example, questions have been raised regarding the reliability and validity of self report data from children regarding sexual matters.

7.13 If self report data from control subjects is difficult to gather, it is scarcely surprising that gathering data from children who have sexually abused is also very difficult. It is widely recognised that perpetrators of sexual abuse are rarely honest about their cognitions and behaviour, at least not without considerable time and effort being expended by interviewers. Whilst there is some evidence that children may be more forthcoming than adults in this respect[4], researchers must anticipate taking meticulous care to ensure that self report data is reliable and valid.

7.14 ***In the light of the above issues, the Committee of Enquiry recommends that government departments, universities, other potential funding bodies, and those agencies undertaking the work, should support and facilitate research as a matter of urgency in the following areas:***

- ***Incidence; there is a need to develop agreed data collection systems across agencies, to ensure comparable data bases, and to give a more systematic overview of how many children and young people need to be worked with. A more comprehensive analysis of the criminal statistics relating to sex offending, looking more closely at the relationship between age and sentence/disposal would provide useful information.***
- ***Intervention Outcomes; which type of treatment methods and approaches are appropriate, with which children and in what circumstances? Pilot centres of research would enable thorough, longitudinal evaluative studies to take place, whereby cases are followed up over a period of time. This would give important information about the meaning of the abuse for both victim and perpetrator, and about the effectiveness of the different interventions.***
- ***Causation; why do young people offend or behave in these ways? What factors aid the process of becoming an adult sex offender, and what factors inhibit it? What is the significance of the personal histories of the young people on their sexual offending patterns?***
- ***Sexuality; what is 'normal' sexual development and knowledge? Why are there so many male abusers? Why do some women abuse?***

7.15 The Committee recognises that progress towards detailed data and firm conclusions regarding the above is likely to be slow and, given the methodological difficulties, perhaps inevitably incomplete. Nevertheless, properly conducted research is the only means of reducing the uncertainties which presently exist.

7.16 ***As well as the need for longitudinal studies to examine the similarities, differences and outcomes in the lives of groups of abusers and treatment approaches, the Committee also recommends that practitioners are encouraged and enabled by those agencies for whom they work, to talk and write more about the work they are doing with young abusers, as this is also an important way of developing a knowledge base.***

7.17 ***Research is also important in terms of informing training. The Committee recommends that those who are involved in training staff to work with young abusers are kept constantly aware of those developments in the field of research which are pertinent to this area of practice.***

Chapter 8: Recommendations

In the light of the work undertaken by the Committee of Enquiry, the following recommendations are made:-

Chapter 2

1) Where there is concern that a child or young person has been involved in sexually abusive behaviour this should be brought to the attention of either the Social Services or the Police, and an investigation should be undertaken.

Chapter 3

1) The Committee commends to all professionals the statement on the use of sexually explicit material in work with adult sex offenders, as developed by ROTA, but recommends that even more care should be taken in work with young abusers. The statement says that all sexually explicit material,

   "to a greater or lesser extent .... can be misused, leading to further abuse, offences and negative role modelling. It is therefore essential that in using any sexually explicit material, practitioners are clear why and how it is being used, and that it (the work) is set in the context of the underlying sexual and social attitudes and power relationships of men towards women and children."

Chapter 4

1. Courts should ensure that, prior to sentencing, they are provided with an assessment of the young person's background of behaviour, and a list of available facilities, and their suitability for different types of cases. This would allow informed decisions to be taken with regard to disposal.
2. As a matter of urgency, the Judicial Studies Board and those responsible for the training of Magistrates should include issues relating to children and young people who abuse other children within their programmes of study.

Chapter 5

1. An overall, systematic approach should be developed for dealing with cases (alleged or otherwise) where a child or young person has abused another child.
2. Each agency involved in work with young perpetrators of sexual abuse should define its specific responsibility in this area of work, within the context of the overall aims and objectives of the organisation, and should develop a clear statement of agency policy in this matter. This includes Social Services, Police, Probation, Education, and Health.
3. Work with children and young people who sexually abuse other children should take place within the context of Child Protection System. All such work should therefore fall under the auspices of the Area Child Protection Committee (ACPC), whose function it would be to co-ordinate the work, bring it into the child protection conference system, and develop a strategic plan.
4. Separate child protection conferences for the victim and the abuser should be organised.
5. Directors of Social Services are recommended to ensure that the whole issue of children and young people who abuse other children is put prominently on the agenda, both of their own agencies and that of the ACPC.
6. All ACPCs should devote a section of their annual report to the work undertaken with children and young people who sexually abuse other children.
7. In recognition of the level of skills and expertise which already exist within the probation service, the Home Office should give urgent consideration to ways in which the Probation Service can strengthen their involvement with young abusers.

8. The police should never NFA a case of a young person who is believed to have sexually abused another child, nor decide to caution, without first contacting, or meeting with social services, and considering the need for a child protection conference to be called. The Home Office should be responsible for drawing such an instruction to the attention of Chief Constables.

9. Reports of children or young people having abused other children should be subject to joint investigation by the Police and Social Services, although this will not necessarily involve joint interviewing.

10. The Home Office should issue strict guidelines regarding the safe-keeping and restricted use of victim statements (including statements made on video), whilst at the same time ensuring appropriate availability to those bona fide professionals who are undertaking the assessment and/or interventions with the alleged or confirmed perpetrators of sexual abuse.

11. A 'continuum of care' should be created, involving a range of agencies working with young perpetrators of sexual abuse. Such a system would make available - on either a legally mandated or voluntary basis - different services ranging from child guidance clinics (who will be in a position to work with children displaying sexually inappropriate behaviours) to secure accommodation offering treatment programmes. The continuum would also include community based treatment programmes with accommodation, community based programmes with the child or young person living at home, or with foster parents, or programmes where the family is enabled to provide support for the young person living in the home.

12. In order to create a 'continuum of care', and to address the need for management and intervention, a network of specific specialist services should be established throughout the UK. The Department of Health and the Home Office should act as 'brokers', facilitating the development of projects and funding the shortfall incurred in the initial opening period. Such projects could well be managed by local authorities or voluntary organisations, as well as health authorities, or the probation service.

13. All agencies establishing projects should require those projects to have a specified programme which identifies the problems to be addressed and the methods to be used, the time-scale, the aims and objectives, and the proposed method of evaluation.

14. All agencies should ensure that in residential settings for children and young people there is access to a telephone which can be used in privacy, and information about how to reach helplines or independent advocates such as ChildLine, NCH Carelines, and the Advocacy Scheme for Children.

15. All Social Service Departments and Voluntary Child Care agencies should ensure that decisions regarding the placement of children in residential care are made on an individual basis, taking into account the nature of the abusive behaviour, the vulnerability of the children or young people living in the establishment, the level of training which the staff have received, the ethos of the establishment, and the resource implications of such a placement. In making decisions about a placement however, the needs of the child or young person who has been involved in abusive behaviour should not take priority over the needs of the other children and young people in the establishment.

16. The Home Office and the Department of Health should ensure that intensive treatment is made available to all young sexual abusers who are in custody.

17. A child or young person who is known to have sexually abused another child should never be placed with foster carers if there are younger, or developmentally less advanced children or young people in the foster placement.

18. Where it is known that a child or young person who is about to be placed with foster carers has exhibited sexually abusive behaviour, the Committee recommends that the placing agency must always fully inform the foster carers of the circumstances.

19. Where it has been established that a child or young person has been involved in sexually abusive behaviour, the school must be informed.

20. The teacher who is normally responsible for liaison with the child protection agencies is the most appropriate person to oversee any involvement with a child or young person who has sexually abused.

21. The Department of Health should ensure that a national information service is established, which would receive details of all projects working with young sex abusers, for the benefit of professionals, courts and carers/parents etc. The Committee believes that there are various options for the organisation of such a network, but suggests the following model as one potential way forward:

    Each project working with young sex abusers should be required to notify the local ACPC of the existence of the service, and the nature of the services provided. ACPCs could then maintain an annually reviewed list of provisions for children and young people who have abused other children. On an annual basis, these lists could be forwarded to the Department of Health, who would have responsibility for compiling an annually updated register of such provision. The DoH would be responsible for disseminating this information.

22. Government departments (Department of Health, Home Office, Department of Education and Science, Lord Chancellor's Department) should be responsible for developing and disseminating nationally agreed guidelines for good practice in relation to work with young abusers, ensuring input from Area Child Protection Committees. Alternatively, the Government could commission a national organisation such as NOTA to do this on its behalf. It is most appropriate that these guidelines emerge from, and are endorsed by, a multi-disciplinary organisation recognised nationally, and with as large a membership as possible.

Chapter 6

1. Training is vital for ALL those working with children and young people who abuse other children. This training should be aimed at:

    - Primary carers (foster carers, residential workers). Often this group tend to be overlooked for training purposes, and training is not seen as a crucial, integral part of the role they play;
    - Specialist Practitioners (including child protection liaison teachers);
    - Supervisors;
    - Senior Management;
    - Members of all ACPCs.

2. Proposals should be drawn up for various levels of training, and should aim to encompass the following areas:

    - An examination of attitudes to abuse and sexuality;
    - The general physical, emotional and sexual development of children;
    - The nature of abusive behaviour and definitions;
    - The development of skills needed to work with young abusers;
    - An overview of existing theory and practice in the field, in recognition that no one theory has the ultimate answer in this work;
    - General experience in working therapeutically with young people;
    - An overview of what can and cannot be achieved through particular therapeutic stances;
    - How to undertake assessments, particularly with regard to risk and future dangerousness;
    - An understanding of the psycho-sexual socialisation of adults, which can lead to attitudes which may be exploited or exploitative – from sociological, feminist and family systems perspectives;
    - The development of skills needed to work in consultation with other professionals;
    - Supervised Practice;
    - Work with people with learning disabilities who display sexually inappropriate behaviour;
    - Work with female sex offenders.

3. ACPCs and their constituent agencies should encourage the development of training in this area of work and ensure that appropriate levels of training are available to all staff working with children and young people who sexually abuse other children. In order to facilitate this, each agency should appoint a lead officer to take responsibility for the development of comprehensive training programmes for staff. The Committee further recommends that CCETSW, the Royal College of Psychiatrists, the British Psychological Society and other training institutions offer and/or specify relevant training for those people likely to encounter or offer a service to young sexual abusers in the course of their professional duties.

4. Managers must recognise, as a matter of urgency, the need for the skilled supervision of staff who are working with young abusers.

5. Managers should ensure that supervision is regular and takes place regardless of the level of experience of the workers.

6. In addition to personal supervision, recognition should be given by managers to organised staff groups within which workers from different disciplines can increase their level of skill and understanding whilst having the opportunity to work through their feelings and anxieties.

7. A thorough audit of skills held by those involved in supervising this work should be conducted by all agencies working with young abusers; training should then be provided where there is a deficit. This may entail a need for external consultancy, and this should be made available where necessary.

Chapter 7

1. Government departments, universities, other potential funding bodies, and those agencies undertaking the work, should support and facilitate research to be undertaken as a matter of urgency in the following areas:

   - Incidence; there is a need to develop agreed data collection systems across agencies, to ensure comparable data bases, and to give a more systematic overview of how many children and young people need to be worked with. A more comprehensive analysis of the criminal statistics relating to sex offending, looking more closely at the relationship between age and sentence/disposal would provide useful information.
   - Intervention Outcomes; which type of treatment methods and approaches are appropriate, with which children and in what circumstances? Pilot centres of research would enable thorough, longitudinal evaluative studies to take place, whereby cases are followed up over a period of time. This would give important information about the meaning of the abuse for both victim and perpetrator, and about the effectiveness of the different interventions.
   - Causation; why do young people offend or behave in these ways? What factors aid the process of becoming an adult sex offender, and what factors inhibit it? What is the significance of the personal histories of the young people on their sexual offending patterns?
   - Sexuality; what is 'normal' sexual development and knowledge? Why are there so many male abusers? Why do some women abuse?

2. Practitioners should be encouraged and enabled by those agencies for whom they work, to talk and write more about the work they are doing with young abusers, as this is also an important way of developing a knowledge base.

3. Those who are involved in training staff to work with young abusers should be kept constantly aware of those developments in the field of research which are pertinent to this area of practice.

Notes

Chapter 1

1. In September 1991, the Regional Offenders Treatment Association (ROTA) became the National Offenders Treatment Association (NOTA). ROTA, a North West based organisation was formed following a conference on working with sex offenders held in 1989. It is an organisation of professionals formed to offer support, consultation and an infrastructure to stimulate development of services for sex offenders. The aims of NOTA remain similar but the group now operates with a national, rather than a regional brief.

Chapter 2

1. Knoth,R., Boyd,K., and Surgen,B., (1988) 'Empirical Tests of Sexual Selection Theory Predictions in Onset, Intensity and Time Course of Sexual Arousal.' Journal of Sex Research, V24, p73-89 and,
   Smith,M., Grocke,M., (in preparation) 'Normal Family Sexuality and Sexual Knowledge in Children.'

Chapter 3

1. Criminal Statistics for England and Wales (1989): HMSO
2. Finkelhor, D., (1979) 'Sexually Victimised Children': Free Press, New York.
3. Horne,L., Glasgow,D., Cox,A., and Calam,R., (1991) 'Sexual Abuse of Children by Children', The Journal of Child Law, V3, no.4 p147-151.
4. Hengeller,S., (1989) 'Delinquency in Adolescence': Sage.
5. Royal Belfast Hospital for Sick Children, and Queen's University Belfast, (1990) 'Child Sexual Abuse in Northern Ireland – A Research Study of Incidence': Greystone Press.
6. Kelly,L., Regan,L., and Burton,S., (1991) 'An Exploratory Study of the Prevalence of Sexual Abuse in a Sample of 16-21 year olds': Polytechnic of North London.
7. Monck,E., Bentovim, A., Goodall, G., Hyde, C., Lwin, R., and Sharland, E. (1992) Child Sexual Abuse: A descriptive and treatment study. Report to the Department of Health: HMSO.
8. Working Together Under the Children Act 1989: A Guide to Arrangements for Inter-agency Co-operation for the Protection of Children from Abuse, (1991): Home Office, Dept. Health, Dept. Education and Science, Welsh Office: HMSO.
9. Kettle, J., (1990) 'Survey of Treatment Facilities for Abused Children and of Treatment Facilities for Young Sexual Abusers of Children': NCH/Dept. of Health.
10. Kelly,L., Regan,L., and Burton,S., (1991) 'An Exploratory Study of the Prevalence of Sexual Abuse in a Sample of 16-21 year olds': Polytechnic of North London.
11. NACRO (1991) 'Seizing the Initiative – NACRO's final report on the DHSS Intermediate Treatment Initiative to Divert Juvenile Offenders form Care and Custody'.
12. Vizard, E., (1991) 'Issues for the Way Ahead' in Bentovim, A., Vizard,E., and Hollows, A., 'Children and Young People as Abusers: An Agenda for Action' (1991), Hollows,A., and Armstrong, H., (eds): NCB.
13. Abel, G.G., Becker, J.V., Mittelman, M., Cunningham-Rathier, J., Rouleau, J., and Murphy, W., (1987) 'Self Reported Sex Crimes in Non-Incarcerated Paraphilias', Journal of Interpersonal Violence, Vol 2. no 1.
14. Behaviour modification should not be confused with approaches which are punitive and/or unethical, such as the 'Pin Down' system which has recently been widely reported in the media.
15. In September 1991, the Regional Offenders Treatment Association (ROTA) became the National Offenders Treatment Association (NOTA). ROTA, a North West based organisation was formed following a conference on working with sex offenders held in 1989. It is an organisation of professionals formed to offer support, consultation and an infrastructure to stimulate development of services for sex offenders. The aims of NOTA remain similar but the group now operates with a national, rather than a regional brief.

16. ROTA (1991) 'The Use of Sexually Explicit Material in Work with Adult Sex Offenders.'
17. Ryan,G., Lane,S.,Davis,J., and Isaac,C., (1987) 'Juvenile Sex Offenders: Development and Correction', Child Abuse and Neglect V11, no.3 p 385-395.
18. SPARK; developed for children under the age of 13 by Kee McFarlane and implemented in 1985. See Cunningham, C., and McFarlane,K., (1991) 'Group Treatment Strategies For Young Sexual Abusers': Safer Society Series no.7.
19. 'It's a Man's World', The B-Team (resources for Boyswork), c/o BCM. B-Team, London WC1 3XX.
20. 'The Grapevine Game': Youth Work Press.
21. NACRO Briefing 'Race and Criminal Justice' (1991).
22. La Fontaine, J., (1991) 'Bullying: The Child's View', ChildLine.
23. Finkelhor, D., (1984) 'Four Pre-Conditions - A Model' in Finkelhor, D., 'Child Sexual Abuse: New Theory and Research': Free Press, New York.
24. Finkelhor,D., and Browne, A., 'Initial and Long-term Effects: A Conceptual Framework' in Finkelhor, D., (1986) 'A Source Book on Child Sexual Abuse': Sage.
25. Cavanagh Johnson, T., (1989) 'Female Child Perpetrators: Children who Molest Other Children', Child Abuse and Neglect V13, no.4 p571-585.
26. Kelly,L., Regan,L., and Burton,S., (1991) 'An Exploratory Study of the Prevalence of Sexual Abuse in a Sample of 16-21 year olds': Polytechnic of North London.
27. Abel, G.G., Becker, J.V., Mittelman, M., Cunningham-Rathier, J., Rouleau, J., and Murphy, W., (1987) 'Self Reported Sex Crimes in Non-Incarcerated Paraphilias', Journal of Interpersonal Violence, Vol 2. no 1.
28. Ryan,G., Lane,S., Davis,J., and Isaac,C., (1987) 'Juvenile Sex Offenders: Development and Correction', Child Abuse and Neglect V11, no.3 p 385-395.
29. Eth, S., and Pynoos,R.S., (1985) 'Post Traumatic Stress Disorder in Children': American Psychiatric Association.
30. Sheber, A., (1985) 'The Penguin Dictionary of Psychology' : Penguin.
31. Goldstein,H., (1981) 'Social Learning and Change, a Cognitive Approach to Human Services': University of Columbia Press.
32. Ryan,G., Lane,S., Davis,J., and Isaac,C., (1987) 'Juvenile Sex Offenders: Development and Correction', Child Abuse and Neglect V11, no.3 p 385-395.
33. Gordon, S., (1973) A Response to Warren Johnson in 'Human Sexuality and the Mentally Retarded', G.D. Lavech(ed) :Rummer/Marvel and,
McNab, W.C., (1978) 'The Sexual Needs of the Mentally Handicapped' in 'Mental Handicap and Sexuality' Ann Craft (1987): Costello.
34. Mitchell, L.K., 'Intervention in the Inappropriate Sexual Behaviour of Individuals with Mental Handicaps', Ann Craft (1987): Costello.

Chapter 4

1. In September 1991, the Regional Offenders Treatment Association (ROTA) became the National Offenders Treatment Association (NOTA). ROTA, a North West based organisation was formed following a conference on working with sex offenders held in 1989. It is an organisation of professionals formed to offer support, consultation and an infrastructure to stimulate development of services for sex offenders. The aims of NOTA remain similar but the group now operates with a national, rather than a regional brief.
2. Webberley,J., (1991) 'Adolescent Sex Offenders' The Journal of Child Law V3, no.4 p152-158.
3. Children and Young Person's (Scotland) Act 1937, s.55; Criminal and Young Person's (Scotland) Act 1975, ss.170,369.
4. Social Work (Scotland) Act 1968, s.32 (2) (g) *Merrin v. S* 1987 SLT 193.

Chapter 5

1. KIDSCAPE (contact: Michelle Eliott), 152 Buckingham Palace Road, London SW1W 9TR.
2. 'All God's Children? Children's Evangelism in Crisis' (1991), A Report from the General Synod Board of Education and Board of Mission: National Society/Church Publishing House.
3. Working Together Under the Children Act 1989: A Guide to Arrangements for Inter-agency Co-operation for the Protection of Children from Abuse (1991): Home Office, Dept. Health, Dept. Education and Science, Welsh Office. HMSO.
4. Police and Criminal Evidence Act 1984.

5. Haaven,J., Little,R., Petre-Miller,D., (1990) 'Treating Intellectually Disabled Sex Offenders: A Model Residential Programme': The Safer Society Press.
6. Sir William Utting (1991), 'Children in the Public Care: A Review of Residential Care': HMSO
7. KIDSCAPE (contact: Michelle Eliott), 152 Buckingham Palace Road, London SW1W 9TR.
8. Working Together Under the Children Act 1989: A Guide to Arrangements for Inter-agency Co-operation for the Protection of Children from Abuse (1991): Home Office, Dept. Health, Dept. Education and Science, Welsh Office: HMSO.
9. In September 1991, the Regional Offenders Treatment Association (ROTA) became the National Offenders Treatment Association (NOTA). ROTA, a North West based organisation was formed following a conference on working with sex offenders held in 1989. It is an organisation of professionals formed to offer support, consultation and an infrastructure to stimulate development of services for sex offenders. The aims of NOTA remain similar but the group now operates with a national, rather than a regional brief.
10. Social Work (Scotland) Act 1968.
11. 'Effective intervention - Child Abuse: Guidance on Co-operation in Scotland' (1989): Scottish Office: HMSO.

Chapter 7

1. Peterson, A., (1988) Annual Review of Psychology, V39, p583-607.
2. O'Hagan, K., (1989) 'Working with Child Sexual Abuse':Open University Press.
3. Knoth, R., Boyd, K., and Surgen, B., (1988) 'Empirical Tests of Sexual Selection Theory Predictions in Onset, Intensity and Time Course of Sexual Arousal.' Journal of Sex Research, V24, p73-89, and Smith, M. Grocke, M., (in preparation) 'Normal Family Sexuality and Sexual Knowledge in Children.'
4. Horne, L., Glasgow, D., Cox, A., and Calam, R., (1991) 'Sexual Abuse of Children by Children', The Journal of Child Law, V3, no.4 p147-151.

APPENDIX 1

System Developed in Shropshire Social Services Dept for Dealing with Young Perpetrators of Sexual Abuse

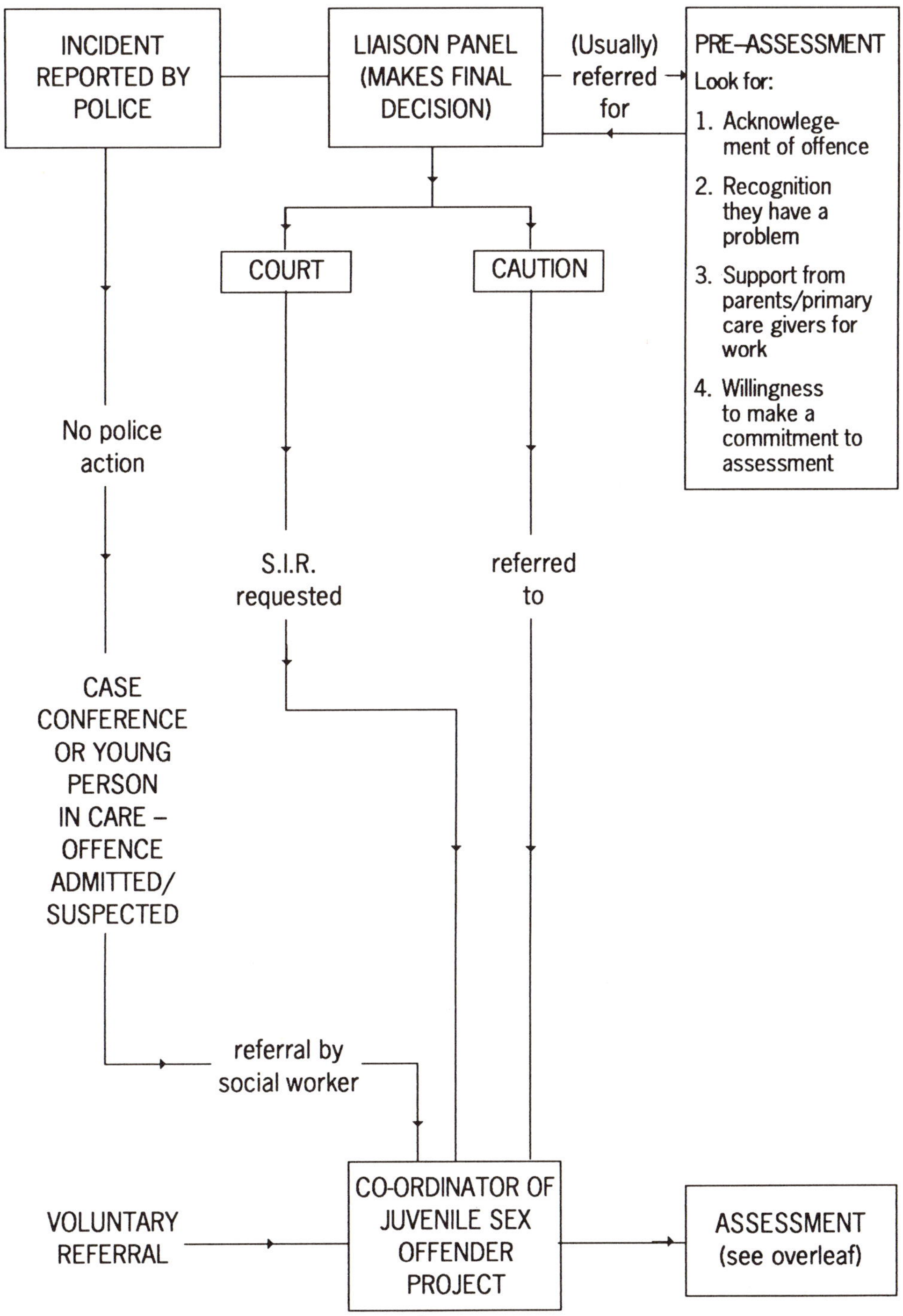

ASSESSMENT

Contract: *(worker/parents/ young person)*	Why For how long Who agrees to what Limited confidentiality
Report:	Who sees it (agreed beforehand)
Sessions:	Six/eight – one/one and a half hours per session, but can be flexible

1. Initial session is information gathering, non-threatening.
2. Give permission to use sexual terms.

   Establish these.

   Initial account of offence(s).
3. If account close to victim/survivor, explore patterns which led to actions/ thoughts/feelings.

   If account differs, begin to challenge.

   Use assumptions of behaviour and other offences.

   Identify denials, excuses, rationalisations and justifications.

IDENTIFY:

Attitudes: Use of questionnaires, 'brainstorm' and discussions.

IDENTIFY:

Fantasies:	Chart of fantasies kept by young person. Explore fantasies.
Offence cycle:	Draw up, check out.
Victim awareness:	How much understanding has abuser of victim's feelings?

For caution assessments more work needed on drawing up 'warning signs', list/actions, etc. Aim to return with this, plus cycle, to parents.

REPORT contains Risk Assessment
+ Suggestions for long-term work if appropriate
+ 'Warning Signs' and high risk situations

Research into Treatment Facilities for Young Sexual Abusers

By Celia Crowe and Judith Kettle

Summary

Methodology

In the Summer of 1991, interviews were carried out with staff working in sixteen different treatment facilities for children and young people known to have sexually abused other children. Using a semi-structured questionnaire, staff were asked to talk about all aspects of their work with young abusers. Those treatment facilities in which interviews were conducted, were classified into one of five different categories:

- i) Hospital based clinics
- ii) Community based clinics
- iii) Community based projects
- iv) Residential Facilities
- v) Groups run by multi-agency and/or multi-professional groups of interested individuals.

Data was obtained from three facilities in each of the categories i), ii), iii), and v), and four facilities in category iv). The treatment facilities within each category represented a wide variety of approaches. This summary draws together the main issues and key messages which emerged from this, essentially descriptive, research. There is no attempt to evaluate the work of the particular facilities which participated.

The quotations cited give an insight into the whole problem of working with children and young people who abuse other children. Problems are described concerning the recognition of abuse, referrals, assessment, treatment and conclusion of treatment. Staff talk about their perceived successes and failures, and they offer advice based on their own experiences to those who wish to embark on this work.

Key Messages

Two themes recurred throughout the interviewing process.

The first related to the emotional and psychological toll that this work has on staff. Staff reported feeling 'dirty', 'distaste', 'despair', 'devalued', and 'isolated'. They found the work 'personally provocative'. Many recognised the need to examine their own sexuality in some depth. However, they expressed the belief that what they were doing was worthwhile, because they believed that it may prevent further abuse and protect potential victims. The research interview was apparently used by some staff to 'offload'; to share their feelings, thoughts and dilemmas. This, in itself, is indicative of staff having few other opportunities to discuss their work and find support. For those who felt unsupported, their frustration and tiredness was beginning to dull their enthusiasm for this work. Such an emotional toll is not surprising in the light of the fact that few facilities had been set up specifically to work with sexual abusers. Rather, the work was carried out in addition to a 'normal' workload, in the context of a project designed to do other types of work.

Staff, however, were pleased that this research was taking place – seeing it as a promising indication that the work was on the agenda nationally. Certainly the frustration experienced did not reflect itself in a reduced commitment to the need for the work to take place. It was hoped that the research might lead to some of the dilemmas and difficulties associated with the work being addressed, that the isolation of staff might be reduced, and that managers might be persuaded to recognise and acknowledge the role of those staff attempting to work with young abusers. The enthusiasm with which the research was met appeared to be a direct result of the problems staff are experiencing in trying to work with young abusers.

The second recurring theme concerned referrals. Doubts certainly existed as to whether referral rates accurately convey the real numbers of children and young people who are involved in abusive behaviours. Staff expressed concern that young people known to be abusing were not being referred to them. Staff had many ideas and gave four main reasons why this should be the case:

1. *Ignorance and lack of recognition of abusing behaviour.*

2. *Denial* – by families who refuse to accept that abuse has occurred, and by professionals who choose to deal with other behavioural problems and ignore the abusing behaviour.

3. *Minimisation* – *"There is a belief ... that in fact sexual abuse is a kind of boyish prank that lads grow out of – boys will be boys', 'sowing wild oats' etc. There is a feeling that minimal intervention is best and it is probably going to be worse if they identify these kids as sexual abusers".* (5)

4. *Collusion* – The idea that *"He only did it once. He says he won't do it again".*

These themes are reminiscent of the difficulties, and consequently of the effects, on referrals of child sexual abuse victims a decade ago.

Research responses indicate that these four factors can exist in all agencies, including the legal profession, at all levels of management, and within society in general. The cumulative effect is that many referrals are not being made, or are being dealt with inappropriately. At the time of the research, lack of policy and procedures considerably exacerbated this situation, although the position was not universal. In some areas the problem of children and young people abusing other children was being addressed by an agency.

If the four factors outlined above are as prevalent as the research suggests, the implication for child protection procedures will be of concern to all. If they are displayed by a participating member, or members, of a multi-agency team charged with child protection, the process of working together will undoubtedly prove to be a difficult task.

The guidance in 'Working Together', (Department of Health, 1991) should, if properly implemented, bring some clarity and help to those who are currently struggling to provide appropriate ways of dealing with abusive behaviour. However, there will be little movement forward unless the policy, procedure and practice guidelines suggested by the D.O.H. are also accompanied by considerable changes in attitude on behalf of professionals and the general public alike.

In addition to these two recurring themes, the research identified a lack of trained workers to offer treatment, a lack of competent supervision for staff working with young abusers, inadequate resources, and insufficient knowledge to evaluate treatment and intervention outcomes or assess for risk of re-abusing.

Results

The following commentary describes the responses of staff to the various themes addressed in the research interview.

Terminology

Staff representing the whole range of agencies and disciplines described difficulties in naming the 'abusive' behaviour of young people. For staff working in a juvenile justice setting, legal terminology was likely to be used:

"The only word we would use is 'sex offender', if they have been through the legal process."

In other settings, the position was less clear.

The uncertainty seemed to become particularly acute when pre-adolescents were involved. The difference in staffs' perceptions of what is actually happening is highlighted by the range of different terms used. Some referred to children who were 'playing sexually with other children' or 'hurting sexually', whilst others referred to 'sexual abusers or offenders'.

The anxiety not to 'label' children has always existed, but labelling someone because of their sexual behaviour is fraught with difficulties in a society that lurches from ideas of 'sexual perverts' to 'boys will be boys'.

Many facilities stressed that it was the behaviour, not the child, which was labelled. One facility offered the comment that labelling could be important - it helped provide the structure to understand the behaviour in order that there could be appropriate provision of services.

Definitions

Six facilities had a specific definition relating to the behaviour of sexually abusing children and young people. The remainder had ideas which could be incorporated into a general working definition.

Some facilities used a legal definition of sexually abusive behaviour. Others drew elements from definitions evolved for child sexual abuse victims; this was particularly the case in those facilities working with a younger age group. Some drew elements from definitions developed to describe adult sex offenders.

None of these definitions, however, appear totally satisfactory.

Use of a legal definition can create a 'two-tier' system with a legal definition for those who are of an age to be held criminally responsible, and another definition for the younger age group. This implies that children younger than the age of criminal responsibility cannot behave in a sexually abusive way. In addition, legal definitions contain no explicit reference to the abuse of power, yet this was a tenet which many interviewees held dear. It also needs to be asked to what extent a legal definition is useful when deciding if treatment is appropriate.

Definitions based upon child sexual abuse victims or adult sex offenders have not in themselves necessarily been critically considered and found helpful. They may have been 'borrowed' simply because of lack of specific discussion or knowledge regarding young sex abusers.

Such a variety of ways of talking about the phenomenon of children and young people who abuse, is problematic because it makes recognition more difficult. If there are no clear definitions, it needs to be asked how others can be educated in recognising abusive behaviour. Some may be reluctant to make a referral if the definition concentrates on the illegality of the abusive behaviour (as with a legal definition). Others may be confused if the definition is the same as that for a victim of abuse.

Hopefully as the knowledge base grows in this area, clearer and more satisfactory definitions will emerge. However, with such a variety of belief systems in existence, concerning children and young people as abusers, it may well prove to be a hard exercise.

Initial Referrals

The research suggested that many abusing youngsters are not being initially referred, largely because of ignorance and denial on the part of those in a position to refer. Many who are referred are referred as *victims* of abuse; their abusive behaviour being viewed as a symptom of their own abuse. Clearly in making referrals, a child's own abuse is seen as a significant factor.

"I can think of a couple of lads who have been referred as victims as opposed to their own abusing behaviour [sic]. If they have been in care, they are more likely to be seen as victims. A lot of social workers deal with abusers in a totally different way if they have been abused."

The ad hoc nature of referral routes was emphasised. One facility summed this feeling up, describing referral routes as "chaotic beyond description".

Much feeling existed that the ethnic, cultural and racial diversity of our society is not being reflected in referrals. No-one was in doubt that this was a distortion, and that young sexual abusers exist throughout society. Various suggestions were made as to why females are rarely referred and as to why proportional numbers of the middle and upper classes and of minority ethnic communities are not being referred. It was believed that middle classes use private resources, that girls are more likely to be put into victim groups, and that a disproportionately high number of males from minority ethnic communities are placed in custodial or secure accommodation.

While referrals of young female sexual abusers are rare, strong feelings were expressed that some women *are* involved in abusive behaviours.

"We are sure they are out there!"

Some respondents reported being aware of female abusers, but suggested that they were not being recognised, or defined as sexual abusers despite their evidently abusive behaviour.

Perhaps it is not surprising that this situation exists given that the general public and professionals alike struggle to accept that adult females sexually abuse.

Assessments and Access To Treatment

All facilities carried out some form of assessment for suitability for treatment.

While secure units had an explicitly defined role of containment, other types of facility accepted youngsters for treatment following an assessment of their potential for change.

It would appear however, that those youngsters who are judged to be unlikely to change, and to whom no appropriate offer of treatment can be made may well 'fall through the net' and be allowed to continue their offending behaviour. Alternative points of referral were not believed to be widely available.

"there isn't anywhere that I know of ..."

"there isn't another local resource ..."

It was apparent that staff were often unaware of other local facilities, and that choices were severely limited. In the absence of alternatives this usually meant youngsters being referred to a secure environment. A few young people were reported as being sent to one of the few specialist facilities available, such as the Aycliffe Centre for Children.

Other staff felt their own project to be 'the end of the road'. This manifested itself in the air of isolation and resignation expressed.

Treatment

The research was undertaken on the basis of a series of logical assumptions:

- that facilities would have an underlying philosophy which would underpin their treatment programme;
- that the treatment programme would follow an assessment;
- that theoretical models of treatment would be used for the treatment programme;
- that training in these models would have been undertaken.

Following on from these assumptions it was also hypothesised that projects would engage in supervision, evaluation, and assessment of risk of re-abuse.

However, the questions relating to these assumptions sometimes caused staff discomfort and in some cases defensiveness,

"You can't get away with anything!"

Connections between the philosophy, models, practice and the origins of the use of models, were, in some cases, very unclear.

Treatment Philosophy

Some staff were very uneasy in attempting to express the treatment philosophy used at their project. Others were more clear, and one team had written their philosophy into their treatment programme.

"Sex offenders must take responsibility for sexual abuse without minimising, externalising, or projecting blame onto others. Manipulation and denial are major behavioural overlays of the offence and the response to discovery. Child sexual abuse is a treatable problem. Treatable is defined as helping the offender learn ways of minimising the risk of re-offence. It does not imply cure. Victims are not responsible for child sexual abuse under any circumstances. That informed age-appropriate consenting sexual relationships are to be encouraged whether homosexual or heterosexual."

This stated philosophy is very similar to many used with adult offenders.

Some staff commented that they recognised the need for a treatment philosophy to help bring clarity to their work.

"... we are still really working through it to get a clear philosophy, because sometimes we have different opinions on the way to work."

The interviews confirmed the need for projects to operate a clear, shared philosophy in a multi-agency, multi-disciplinary team; a philosophy which specifically relates to work with young sexual abusers, rather than a philosophy which makes general statements about children or childcare. Without such a philosophy a young abuser is likely to experience contradiction and inconsistencies of treatment which can only reduce the effectiveness of treatment programmes.

Theoretical models

Using a checklist of theoretical models, staff stated which models were used within their project.

Some staff obviously had an in-depth knowledge of theoretical models of treatment on which to base treatment programmes. Those trained in psychiatry or psychology tended to be more at ease when describing the model they used.

Others, however, experienced considerable difficulty in focusing on and explaining their practice. As the knowledge, understanding and application of treatment models to practice is a fundamental issue which relates closely to a treatment philosophy, this difficulty is perhaps not surprising, bearing in mind the previously described confusion which existed with regard to treatment philosophy. However, without this fundamental understanding of practice, the validity of the treatment itself must be questioned.

Various facilities used an eclectic model of treatment which is,

"... eclectic due to the multi-faceted nature of the problem. It is an individualised treatment programme. Elements are chosen according to ... individual needs."

An eclectic model attempts to redress what some see as the overall lack of a working model.

"We do not believe this area of sexually abusing behaviour has begun to be well enough charted yet for us to have a theoretical model ...".

On the other hand, the use of an eclectic model possibly highlights the lack of knowledge or training of some practitioners. It certainly needs to be asked whether those staff who feel that they have had little training, have the skills necessary to marry models in an appropriate way. Is an eclectic model a 'cop out' or a genuine process towards a new working model of treatment, or both?

There are further issues to be considered with regard to theoretical models. Whilst it has not been argued that work with young abusers should be the exclusive province of any one agency or discipline, problems were reported where attempts had been made to combine different approaches.

"I bought psycho-analytical or analytical Jungian ideas to it (the group). My co-worker brought cognitive-behavioural and psycho-educational models. At the outset we felt that we were poles apart. It took us a long time before we started the group, but the group benefited from the diversity of our approaches. At the end we incorporated some of each others, so that it didn't feel like a split."

This facility had clearly taken time to integrate several different approaches.

Another facility pointed out,

"It can be very difficult because some people here work in an intuitive psychotherapeutic way, others in a more cognitive way. I think there has to be a lot of planning."

It needs to be asked however, whether all facilities have the resources, or the theoretical knowledge to plan in this way, particularly as some models may be incompatible. For example, there has been much debate surrounding combining a feminist perspective and a family therapy approach. Would proponents of behavioural therapy be comfortable with a psychodynamic model?

In view of the numbers of models people said they were using, there has to be some doubt as to whether staff have had sufficient training in their professional lives to be competent in so many models of treatment. This is particularly pertinent when some of the models derive from very different theoretical approaches. It is, however, possible for a team with a sound knowledge of different models to offer a coherent programme. If, however their knowledge is rudimentary, this can only bring, at the very least, confusion to those being treated.

Treatment methods

In those facilities working with adolescents, there seemed to be a tendency to use group work for dealing with a young person's abusive behaviour and to use individual work for dealing with the perpetrator as a victim. For younger children individual work was preferred all round.

The decision about what treatment to offer was based on several factors, with the emphasis being on an assessment and discussion to determine needs. Other factors were the availability of staff, and time available to them to work with the young person.

"We look and see whether we have the bodies available to do it. It is dependent on resources."

The length of treatment programmes varied considerably from facility to facility. In some settings, a group runs for a set period, in others it is more open-ended.

Termination of treatment programme

Decisions regarding the termination of a treatment programme were generally discussed in terms of time factors or resources. One facility commented,

"I don't think that we are aware enough of when and how to terminate the programme. I suppose we base it on a gut feeling at this stage that we cannot do anymore; we have achieved all we can."

Although it might appear to be crucial, only in some instances was termination related to an evaluation of risk. As one facility put it,

"There is a whole range of things we would be reviewing with them before actually saying that treatment could be concluded ... Things we would be looking at are, whether they have made age-appropriate relationships, and maybe gone on to have girlfriends and some sexual experience that was not abusive; looking at their families, their isolation and if they can accept full responsibility without any further hedging or denial about what they have done. If they are clear in their minds about what is abusive and what isn't. And it is about their openness to us."

Formal evaluation of treatment outcome

There were a noticeable lack of formal evaluation procedures in many facilities.

"We have had thoughts but have never had the time or personnel to think very seriously about this ... in a way it is quite difficult, because if we try to get more resources we have very little to prove that what we might offer is effective."

Others evaluated as an ongoing process.

"We evaluate on a week to week basis. What was the kid like at point A? What were they like at point B?"

For a few, the problem was that they did not know how to evaluate. Those who were not evaluating readily acknowledged that this should be done, and were anxious that it was not happening.

"It is one of our priorities. I think it is something that we should address."

Many had plans for the future.

"We are hoping to use other agencies to evaluate what has been happening over the years that the project has been in existence. Re-offending rates are very easy to pick out. I would like to connect with the local university or research in our own department to look at this. We don't want to get into something that is very bland like re-offending rates."

Several facilities experienced specific difficulties with evaluating youngsters with special needs.

Staff found the evaluation of a young person's risk of re-abusing to be a problem. Some felt the need for a 'risk assessment profile'. Very few had reached the stage of formal risk assessment. Of those who had reached this stage, some had a clear sense of risk factors,

"... we have just developed a risk assessment protocol based upon Jonathan Russell's material in the USA. We have adapted it to our needs."

others relied on a gut feeling,

"... we have had several where we have had said loud and clear (that we are worried about these kids) but that is about as close as we come to evaluation."

Without an evaluation process there must be doubts about the success of treatment, and the future risk of the young person re-offending. Whilst projects were reluctant to speak in terms of a 'cure', there was some belief that the risk of re-offending could be reduced.

"We try to have some sort of objective and self-assessment both at the beginning and at the end of the group. I think certainly on a subjective level it is fair to say that we wouldn't feel that any of the boys were no risk ..."

Treating the 'Victim' as well as the Abuser

Staff were asked whether or not they deemed it appropriate to be involved in work with both young abusers and victims. Some staff felt that involvement in both types of work is necessary in order to avoid polarities. Others, however, recognised that they may feel persecutory towards abusers if they work with victims as well. Others expressed a need to work with victims in order to prevent themselves from colluding with the abusers, and to keep themselves 'in touch' with victim issues.

Staff were also asked about working with a young person who is both a victim of sexual abuse and a sexual abuser. They were asked whether or not they believed the two elements could be addressed together, or whether they required different ways of working. It appears that, with older youngsters, the fear of excusing the abusive behaviour, by dealing with the victim aspect negates the possibility of the abusing and abused elements of the behaviour being addressed side by side in treatment. Some facilities have dealt with this by separating out these two issues and having different timetables when each issue is dealt with.

"Treat the abusing behaviour first, except in individual work. Even when they are talking about their victimisation, you make sure that it is not an excuse for their abusing. They chose to abuse – that is the message that they get from us."

Others have different views,

"Staff see no difference in approach to treatment, and do not prioritise the area of work."

"It is a debate that we haven't worked out, whether we want to address the victimisation first. But the problem is we could use that as a way of justifying and minimising his behaviour... Yes, we would focus on the offence... But sometimes you don't get a choice in the matter. In some young people ... if you don't deal with the victim, you are not going to get any further forward."

Certainly it appears that with the younger child, who is more likely to be referred as a victim, there are possibilities of addressing the perpetrator and the victim elements at the same time. The issue of child protection was also relevant here; confusion existed as to whether or not a child protection conference should focus on the child's abusive behaviour, or the child's own abuse, or both?

In conclusion, staff indicated experiencing great stress in trying to strike a balance between challenging the youngster to confront his abusive behaviour, at the same time as taking account of the fact that he may also have been a victim of abuse.

Mandated or Voluntary Treatment?

Some facilities reported that they only worked with youngsters when they had a mandate to do so. However, there was evidence of this causing a certain amount of conflict for staff in Juvenile Justice schemes. Their ethos, traditionally, is to keep youngsters out of courts. However, some respondents working in this context felt the need for a legal mandate in order to keep a young abuser in a treatment programme - although one facility did point out that even with a court order there is no guarantee of engaging the youngster in treatment. Staff in some facilities feared that the courts would view this type of offending very punitively, forcing the youngster up the sentencing tariff - with the risk of the youngster receiving a custodial sentence with perhaps no treatment opportunities.

The alternative to having a legal mandate was felt to be the offer of voluntary treatment. This was felt, however, to bring its own dilemmas. It is widely accepted that most abusing youngsters will minimise the significance of their behaviours and maybe deny them totally . Staff reported that other professionals and families sometimes collude with this attitude, resulting in the child's withdrawal from therapy. This result was felt to be even further complicated if Child Protection procedures had not been used. Some staff felt that such a situation could leave workers with a dilemma; the young person has withdrawn from therapy, yet they suspect that the young person's offending behaviour may continue. Censure from adults was seen to be important in providing young people with the motivation to stop offending.

Working Together

The study revealed that multi-agency and multi-disciplinary co-operation occurs in work with young abusers, particularly at the grass roots level, with varying degrees of success. However, this co-operation appeared to be predominantly initiated by individual workers rather than being sanctioned and supported by management.

Child Protection

Where work with young abusers is concerned, the research suggests a need for the Social Services Inspectorate and Area Child Protection Committees to address Child Protection issues. A wide divergence of practice was reported, ranging from child protection conferences being held as a matter of course at the young abusers point of entry into the Child Protection system, to no child protection conference being held at all.

"The truth of the matter is that we do have procedures in relation to Schedule One offenders, but I have to say that even there, where the young people are in our care, they are not exhaustively followed."

For some staff the protection of the victim, other family members or peers was seen as being paramount. For others, the protection of the young abuser and his/her need for care and protection was seen as paramount.

"We have been grappling with this as it is very ad hoc. Some boys are automatically case conferenced under the child protection procedures, as there are concerns that they may be victims themselves. Others are not."

For other staff, concerns for both these groups were seen to be equally important.

Whilst Child Protection might have been expected to be of crucial importance in this work, the research actually suggested that practice varies enormously with regard to the importance placed upon child protection issues.

A particular difficulty appeared to exist in Health Authorities, where Child Protection procedures were reported as being bypassed, on occasions, and the child placed directly in therapy. One clinical facility put the point,

"... we may say to GPs that they must involve the Social Services and then come back to us, and we hear no more ..."

Some psychiatrists were also reported to treat young abusers without recourse to Child Protection procedures.

With regard to child protection, concern was also expressed about the practice of placing young abusers in a residential setting where there is no treatment on offer. How could they be protected from re-offending?. How could other vulnerable children in that residential setting be protected, some of whom may well have been acting out sexually because they have themselves been abused?

Resources

Work with young abusers was, for various reasons, recognised as having specific resourcing implications:

- In some facilities it is compulsory practise for staff to work in pairs in treatment sessions with young abusers, and staff in many facilities stressed the importance of a male/female staff mix.

- The need for staff to reflect the ethnic background of young people was also recognised.
- Specialist workers were seen as being necessary for work with young abusers. It was felt that these staff should have been specifically trained in this field, to offer a recognised specialised resource.
- Groupwork with young abusers, (which seemed to be the preferred therapeutic response), requires physical space which is sometimes difficult to locate. Effective groupwork involves many hours of planning and preparation on the part of workers and group members.
- Complimentary groupwork with young abusers and their carers or social work staff was reported to be beneficial to both staff and youngsters. The group process was believed to be a powerful way of adding a new dimension to treatment. However, such groupwork, if not properly planned, resourced and supervised, was acknowledged as being potentially quite dangerous for all concerned.

Training

Among the teams and individuals interviewed, the diversity of levels of training and skills, experience and interests was striking. Neither were staff necessarily trained or experienced in the area of child sexual abuse and abuse perpetrated by children or young people.

Some workers had had little professional training in theoretical treatment models and approaches, and little training at all in treating young sexual abusers.

"But honestly and truly my training was not much more than being a social worker. I don't think that any of us could say that we have had specialist training."

Most felt the absence of training keenly. They relied on what they had read, what they felt comfortable with, and the courses offered by known experts such as Ray Wyre and Stephen Wolf.

"Nobody has gone off and done intensive training. Everyone here is a qualified social worker or youth worker. People have been on courses, but we aren't sure you can call two and a half days at Gracewell [Ray Wyre] or two days at a hospital, training. There has been no coherent plan devised that looks at training people who are engaged in this work."

Some were dismayed to discover that being on a course for three days made them their department's 'expert', and training others was now part of their work.

Some respondents talked about training that they had received in child sexual abuse or in treating adult sex offenders. However, it was recognised that there are difficulties in transferring aspects of adult offender programmes to work with young offenders, given the stage they are at in their psychological development.

Some staff recognised that little training was currently available to prepare people for working with young sexual abusers.

"One of the things that we found when we were looking for training for ourselves was that there wasn't any ... We are gathering bits from other people's research, but basically we have had to start from scratch."

However, teams in secure treatment facilities with staff with medical backgrounds, or psychology and teaching qualifications (ie, not social workers) appeared to have greater access to resources for post qualifying training.

Overall, the struggle of staff was apparent. Many made it clear that they were aware of the shortcomings in their training. Many felt thwarted in their attempts to improve this situation, owing to an acknowledged lack of resources (primarily money and time), the low priority place on the work, and the attitudes of management. Some were undertaking training in their own time using their own finances.

Multi-agency and multi-disciplinary training will be crucial in offering a co-ordinated and coherent service to young abusers. Such a programme would also overcome some of the difficulties inherent in the differing approaches and perspectives, which are currently being used.

As interviews were only undertaken with one or two members of each staff team, it is acknowledged that comprehensive details regarding the training of all the staff in the facilities may not have been collected. Some staff could not answer for their colleagues. However, it is clear that there are certain implications for teamwork and team building if some members were not aware of the qualifications, training and experience of their colleagues.

Supervision

The research highlighted the importance of sensitive supervision, as a means of helping to integrate approaches and different perspectives within a multi-disciplinary team.

Most social work interviewees reported that they received line-management supervision. Although this was usually on a regular basis, the lack of specific knowledge or training on the part of the supervisors was clearly felt to be problematic. Consequently, supervisors were not necessarily believed to comprehend the training needs, the need for support, or the emotional needs of their workers. The following quotation from a supervising manager made this point succinctly,

"We do have supervision but we don't have specialist supervision ... because the supervisor needs training and the experience of working in this field - the supervisor has not got any experience. ... we can't respond to the needs that staff have, and we are unable to do that because we are not equipped to do it."

Whilst this opinion of the supervisory process appeared fairly consistent among social work staff, staff working in non-social work disciplines, (where supervision may have different meanings), gave more varied responses with regard to the issues of supervision. For example, staff in one facility described a voluntary fortnightly workshop,

"... which is attended voluntarily ... all the staff here are trained. No-one requires supervision."

A second said,

"... we always have a supervisor for every case."

A third said of supervision,

"There isn't any."

Some staff reported supervising themselves in spite of all the inherent dangers of subjectivity, collusion and insularity that this involves. Others made it clear that they gained support from each other, and this was believed to satisfy the needs that a formal supervisory process could meet.

Overall, staff were dissatisfied with the level of supervision and support they received. They indicated that they wanted individual and team support, which would address professional and personal issues around this work. Clearly, supervision for its own sake is not sufficient; supervision needs to be undertaken by people who are knowledgeable about the issues of abusive behaviour and the impact the work has on staff members.

Overview

The enthusiasm, energy, commitment, and feeling of pride of staff for the work they undertake with young abusers was evident.

"We like the boys in the group. We are enthusiastic and committed to it. Having the groups for the carers at the same time (worked well). We had virtually 100% attendance for 14 weeks."

"We engage the young person ... we try to separate the behaviour from the young person, without reducing their responsibility for their actions. I also think we confront quite well. We are challenging in a way that doesn't make the young person feel as if they are bad – it is just the offences that they have done that are bad."

However, staff were able to identify some of the aspects of their work which had proved difficult for them, and their commitment to 'getting things right' was displayed in a great willingness to face the issues involved.

"Personally sometimes I get too confrontational, too punitive. It is about going over the top in not colluding ... intellectually I have this thing that it doesn't help to persecute perpetrators ..."

Many staff had plans for the future of their work with young abusers. In particular, they wanted training and education, they wanted to develop group work and emphasised their wish to begin to evaluate the work that they were doing. Others had a more global approach.

"Yes we are developing a new facility for them (young abusers). We are currently researching our work with them. We are proposing to expand that to out-patient facilities. We are going to be undertaking a national training course with other people in the UK ... to bring people together who are knowledgeable and interested ... to try to reduce some of the current chaos that exists is this particular area, to something resembling some kind of coherent work. And for a change we are ahead of the Americans!"

When asked to reflect upon the problems of working with sexually abusing children and young people, staff particularly talked about the impact of working in this particular area.

"For any worker it is very difficult working with these boys. You are not there to put them down, to criticise them or in any way to judge them. It is very difficult when you know what offence they have committed and when they are talking about their victims in a very unfeeling way. You do come away sometimes feeling the weight of what they have dumped on you. The other problem is not seeing them as victims because they do present very much as victims themselves, but it is not being seduced into that. Handling the knowledge of the offences some of them have done is pretty gruesome. Looking at what they do I feel angry at times ... a lot of them are self damaging and suicidal risks and you carry that with you, and that is why I say people working with them need caring for themselves."

The advice that staff would offer to other people who were about to embark on work with young abusers varied a great deal. Advice ranged from the need for self examination, training and planning, to the importance of objectivity.

One facility advised potential workers to,

"Get your act together. Set yourselves up properly. Make sure your work is scrutinised closely."

Another said,

"Don't get overwhelmed by it. Have a go at what you think you can do. Learn and work from there."

Whilst such pieces of advice are not necessarily contradictory, they are indicative of the different ways in which positive work with young abusers has developed, and the different structural frameworks within which people are working.

The Final Comment

Regardless of theoretical approach, adherence to specific treatment models, or professional backgrounds, all participants underlined the complexity of the issue of young sexual abusers - at societal, social, political, emotional, moral and ethical levels, as well as in terms of agency provision, referral systems, staff support, training and development.

It is clearly a complex phenomenon which requires a response on many levels; a response which is informed by research and evaluation. The research was met with wide approval from those people who were interviewed. This response in itself, can be seen as a clear indication of the concern and interest which is being expressed about the ways in which work with young abusers is being developed.

"I am very concerned about this population [of young sexual abusers] and actually the lack of things that are organised for them. So that if your research enables the Department of Health to take this on as a priority, that's what will be in it for me ... I hope your Project is successful. It's very hard to sit here and do nothing, because you've got other kids who are going to be abused."

Bibliography

This bibliography is presented in three parts. Part A includes material specifically on the subject of children and young people who abuse other children. Part B includes other directly related material (eg, on the subjects of child sexual abuse or sexual offending). Part C includes other material which may be of interest to the reader.

Part A

Abel, G., & Becker, J.V., "Sexual Interest Card Sort", *Treating Child Sex Offenders and Victims – A Practical Guide* by A.C. Salter (Ed), Sage Pub. Inc.,

Adelson, J. (Ed), *Handbook of Adolescent Psychology,* "The Development of Sexuality in Adolescence" by P.Y. Miller & W. Simon, Wiley & Son, N.Y., 1980.

Ageton, S.S., *Sexual Assault Amongst Adolescents,* Lexington Books, 1983.

Appathurai, C. & Lowery, G., "Young Sex Offenders Need Early Intervention", *OAPSW Newsmagazine,* 3, November, 1985.

Atcheson, J. & Williams, D., "A Study of Juvenile Sex Offenders", *American Journal of Psychiatry,* V.111, p.366-370, 1954.

Awad, G., Saunders, E., & Levene, J., "A Clinical Study of Male Adolescent Sexual Offenders", *International Journal of Offender Therapy and Comparative Criminology,* Vol.28, p.105-116, 1984.

Becker, J.V., Cunningham-Rathner, J. & Kaplan, M.S., *The Adolescent Sexual Perpetrator,* New York State Psychiatric Institute, N.Y., 1984.

Becker, J., Cunningham-Rathner, J. & Kaplan, M., "Adolescent Sex Offenders : Demographics, Criminal and Sexual Histories, and Recommendations for Reducing Future Offences, *Journal of Interpersonal Violence,* 1, p.431-445, 1986.

Becker, J.V., Kaplan, M.S., Cunningham-Rathner, J., & Kavoussi, R., "Characteristics of Adolescent Sexual Perpetrators: Preliminary Findings", *Journal of Family Violence,* 1, p.85-97., 1986.

Becker, J.V., & Abel, G.G. "Methodological and Ethical Issues in Evaluating and Treating Adolescent Sexual Offenders", *Adolescent Sex Offenders: Issues in Research and Treatment,* Research Monograph, US National Centre for the Prevention and Control of Rape, Department of Health and Human Services, Washington, DC, Pub. No. ADM 85-1396, 1985.

Becker, J.V. & Able, G.G., *Methodological and Ethical Issues in Evaluating and Treating Adolescent Offenders,* US Department of Health and Human Services, 1985.

Bengis, S., *A Comprehensive Service-Delivery System with a Continuum of Care for Adolescent Sex Offenders,* Safer Society Press, Orwell, Vermont, 1987.

Bentovim, A., *Children and Young People as Abusers,* Hospital for Sick Children, Great Ormond Street and Tavistock Clinic, London, Paper presented at Conference organised by TAGOSAC and Childline on Children and Young People as Abusers on March 1990., 1990.

Bentovim, A. & Ratner, H., *Focal Family Therapy with the Family of an Adolescent Offender,* 1990.

Bethea-Jackson, G., Chapman-Brissett, S., "The Juvenile Sex Offender: Challenges to Assessment for Outpatient Intervention", *Child and Adolescent Social Work Journal,* No.6, p.127-137, Summer 1989.

Bolton, F.G., Laner, R.H. & Kane, S.F., "Child Maltreatment Risk Among Adolescent Mothers: A Study of Reported Cases", *American Journal of Orthopsychiatry,* V.50, p.489-504, 1980.

Breer, W., *The Adolescent Molester,* Charles C. Thomas Publisher, USA, 1987.

Bremer, J.F., *Adolescent Incest Offenders' Self Concept,* University of Minnesota, Minneapolis, M.N., 1984.

Brooks-Gunn, J. & Furstenburg, F., "Adolescent Sexual Behaviour", *American Psychologist,* V.44, No.2, p.249-257, 1989.

Cantwell, H.B., "Child Sexual Abuse : Very Young Perpetrators", *Child Abuse and Neglect,* V.12, p.579-582, 1988.

Cardozo, M. & Hamblion, M., "A Group for Adolescent Offenders", (Unpublished paper, 1992).

Cole, E., "Sibling Incest: The Myth of Benign Sibling Incest", *Women and Therapy,* The Haworth Press Inc., V.3, p.79-89, 1982.

Constantine, L.L. & Martinson, F.M., *Children and Sex: New Findings, New Perspectives,* "Effects of Early Sexual Experiences: A Review and Synthesis of Research" by L. Constantine, Little, Brown, Boston, 1980.

Davies, T., "Juvenile Sex Offenders", *Association for Juvenile Justice,* p.8-10, Feb 1990.

Davis, G.E., & Leitenberg, H., "Adolescent Sex Offenders", *Psychological Bulletin,* 101, p.417-427, 1987.

De Jong, A.R., "Sexual Interaction Among Siblings and Cousins: Experimentation or Exploitation?", *Child Abuse and Neglect,* V.13, p.271-279, 1989.

Deisher, R.W., Wenet, G.A., Paperny, D.M., Clark, T.F., & Fehrenbach, P.A., "Adolescent Sex Offence Behaviour: The Role of the Physician", *Journal of Adolescent Health Care,* 2, p.279-286, 1982.

Doshay, L., *The Boy Sex Offender and His Later Career,* Grune and Stratton, N.Y., 1943.

Dube, R., Herbert, M., "Sexual Abuse by Children under 12 years of Age: A Review of 511 Cases", *Child Abuse and Neglect,* V.12, p.321-330, 1988.

Fagan, J. & Wexler, S., "Explanations of Sexual Assault Among Violent Delinquents", *Journal of Adolescent Research,* 3, p.363-385, 1988.

Fehrenbach, P.A., Smith, W., Monastersky, C. & Deisher, R.W., "Adolescent Sex Offenders: Offender and Offence Characteristics", *American Journal of Orthopsychiatry,* 56, p.225-233, 1986.

Fehrenbach, P., & Monastersky, C., "Characteristics of Female Adolescent Sexual Offenders, *American Journal of Orthopsychiatry,* V.58 (1), p.148-151., 1988.

Fehrenbach, P.A., Smith, W., Monastersky, C. & Deisher, R.W., "Adolescent Sexual Offence Behaviour", *Journal of Adolescent Health Care,* V.2, p.279-286, 1982.

Fillmore, A., "Treatment of the Juvenile Sex Offender", *Health Visitor,* V.60, p.97-98, March, 1987.

Finklehor, D., "Sex Among Siblings: A Survey Report on its Prevalence, Its Variety and Its Effects", *Archives of Sexual Behaviour,* V.9, p.171-194, 1980.

Gilby, R., Wolf, L., Goldberg, B., "Mentally Retarded Adolescent Sex Offenders: A Survey and Pilot Study", *Canadian Journal of Psychiatry,* No.34, p.542-548, Aug 1989.

Green, D., "Adolescent Exhibitionists: Theory and Therapy", *Journal of Adolescence,* The Association for the Psychiatric Study of Adolescents, V.10, p.45-56, 1987.

Green, D., *Adolescent Exhibitionists,* Paper presented at Scottish branch B.P.S. Annual Meeting, Bridge of Allan, 1984.

Groth, A.N., Hobson, W.F., Lucey, K.P. & St. Pierre, J., "Juvenile Sex Offenders: Guidelines for Treatment", *International Journal of Offender Therapy and Comparative Criminology,* 25, p.265-272, 1981.

Groth, A.N. & Loredo, C.M., "Juvenile Sex Offenders: Guidelines for Assessment", *International Journal of Offender Therapy and Comparative Criminology,* 25, p.31-39, 1981.

Groth, A.N., "The Adolescent Sexual Offender and His Prey", *International Journal of Offender Therapy and Comparative Criminology,* 21, p.249-254, 1977.

Hains, A.A., Herrman, L.P., Baker, K.L. & Graber, S., "The Development of a Psycho-Educational Group Program for Adolescent Sex Offenders", *Journal of Offender Counselling Services and Rehabilitation,* V.11, No.1, p.63-76, 1986.

Halleck, S.L. ,"Voyeurism and Exhibitionism in Adolescence", *Medical Aspects of Human Sexuality*, 9, p.75-76, 1975.

Heinz, J.W., Gargaro, S. & Kelly, K.G., *A Model Residential Juvenile Sex Offenders – The Hennepin County Home School*, Safer Society Series – No.3, Safer Society Press, 3049 East Genesse Street, Syracuse, New York, 13224, 1987.

Henderson, English, MacKenzie, "Family Centred Casework Practice with Sexually Aggressive Children", *Journal of Social Work and Human Sexuality*, V.7, No.2, p.89-108, 1988.

Hoghughi, M. & Richardson, G., "The Legal Sanction", *Community Care*, p.21-23, 1 Nov 1990.

Hoghughi, M. & Richardson, G., "The Root of the Problem", *Community Care*, p.22-24, 25 Oct 1990.

Holt, J., et al, *Picking Up the Pieces: Sexual Abuse and the Juvenile Justice System*, Practice Development and Publications Unit, Leeds: Hilltop Project, Leeds, 1989.

Horne, L., Glasgow, D., Cox, A., Calam, R., "Sexual Abuse of Children by Children", *The Journal of Child Law*, Frank Cass & Co, London, V.3, No.4, p.147-151, Sept-Dec 1991.

Hsu, L.K.G. & Starzynski, J., "Adolescent Rapists and Adolescent Child Sexual Assaulters", *International Journal of Offender Therapy and Comparative Criminology*, 34, p.23-30, 1990.

Hunner, R.J. & Walder, Y.E. (Eds), *Exploring The Relationship Between Child Abuse and Delinquency*, "Perspectives on the Juvenile Sex Offender" by G.A. Wenet, T.R. Clark & G. White, Allanheld, Osmun and Company, Montclair, N.J., p.145-151, 1981.

Jackson, I., *A Preliminary Survey of Adolescent Sex Offences in New York : Remedies and Recommendations*, Safer Society Press, Syracuse, N.Y., 1983.

Johnson, T. Cavanagh, "Female Child Perpetrators - Children Who Molest Other Children: Preliminary Findings", *Child Abuse and Neglect*, V.12, p.219-229, 1988.

Johnson, T., Berry, C., "Children Who Molest: A Treatment Program", *Journal of Interpersonal Violence*, V.4, No.2, p.185-203, 1989.

Johnson, T.C., "Female Child Perpetrators - Children Who Molest Other Children", *Child Abuse and Neglect*, V.13, p.571-585, 1989.

Kahn, T., "Training Staff in the Treatment of Adolescent Sexual Offenders", *Interchange*, Cooperative Newsletter of the Adolescent Perpetrator Network, Denver, CO, p.8-13, 1986.

Kahn, T.J. & Lafond, M.A., "Treatment of the Adolescent Sex Offender", *Child and Adolescent Social Work*, 5, p.135-148, 1988.

Kaplan, M.S., "Characteristics of Parents of Adolescent Incest Perpetrators: Preliminary Findings", *Journal of Family Violence*, V.3, No.3, p.193-191., 1988.

Katz, R., "Psychological Adjustment in Adolescent Child Molesters", *Child Abuse and Neglect*, V.14, p.567-575, 1990.

Kavoussi, R.J., Kaplan, M. & Becker, J.V., "Psychiatric Diagnoses in Adolescent Sex Offenders", *Journal of the American Academy of Child and Adolescent Psychiatry*, V.27, p.241-243, 1988.

Kelly, L, Regan, L. & Burton, S., *An Exploratory Study of the Prevalence of Sexual Abuse in a Sample of 16-21 Year Olds*, Report for ESRC, Child Abuse Studies Unit, The Polytechnic of North London, 1991.

Kettle, J., *Survey of Treatment Facilities for Abused Children and of Treatment Facilities for Young Sexual Abusers of Children*, National Children's Home, London, 1990.

Knopp, F.H., Rosenberg, J. & Stevenson, W., *Report on Nationwide Survey of Juvenile and Adult Sex Offender Treatment Programs and Providers*, Safer Society Press, N.Y., 1986.

Knopp, F.H. & Stevenson, W.F., *Nationwide Survey of Juvenile and Adult Sex Offender Treatment Programs and Models*, Safer Society Program, Orwell, VT 05760-9756, 1988.

Knopp, F.H., *The Youthful Sex Offender : The Rationale and Goals of Early Intervention and Treatment*, Safer Society Press, Syracuse, N.Y., 1985.

Knopp, F.H., *Remedial Intervention in Adolescent Sex Offences,* 1985.

Knopp, F.H., *Remedial Intervention in Adolescent Sex Offences : Nine Program Descriptions,* Safer Society Program of the New York State Council of Churches, New York, 1982.

Kourany, R.F.C., Gwinn, M. & Martin, J.E., "Adolescent Babysitting: A Thirty Year Phenomenon", *Adolescence,* 15, p.939-945, 1980.

Kourany, R.F.C., Martin, J.E., & Armstrong, S.H., "Sexual Experimentation by Adolescents while Babysitting", *Adolescence,* 14, p.283-288, 1979.

Kourany, R.F.C., Martin, J.E. & LaBarbera, J.D., "Adolescents as Babysitters", *Adolescence,* 15, p.155-158, 1980.

Lane, S. & Samora, P., "A Method for Treating the Adolescent Sex Offender", *Dispositional Alternatives for the Juvenile Offender,* Washington, Nov, 6-9, 1983.

Leitenberg, H., Greenwald, E. & Tarran, M., "The Relation Between Sexual Activity Among Children During Preadolescence, Early Adolescence and Sexual Behaviour and Sexual Adjustment in Young Adulthood", *Archives of Sexual Behaviour,* V.18, No.4, p.299-313, 1989.

Lewis, D.O., Shancock, S.S. & Pincus, J.H., "Juvenile Male Sexual Assaulters", *American Journal of Psychiatry,* 136, p.1194-1196, 1979.

Longo, R.E. & Groth, A.N., "Juvenile Sexual Offences in the Histories of Adult Rapists and Child Molesters", *International Journal of Offender Therapy and Comparative and Comparative Criminology,* 27, p.150-155, 1983.

Longo, R. & McFadin, B., "Sexually Inappropriate Behaviour : Development of the Sexual Offender", *Law and Order,* December, p.21-23, 1981.

Longo, R.E., "Sexual Learning and Experience Among Adolescent Sexual Offenders", *International Journal of Offender Therapy and Comparative and Comparative Criminology,* V.26 No.3, p.235-242, 1982.

Maclay, D.T., "Boys Who Commit Sexual Misdemeanours", *British Medical Journal,* 11, p.186-190,1960.

Madanes, C., *Systemic Approaches to Adolescent Offenders and Families* – Presentation to Institute of Family Therapy, London, 1989.

Malamuth, N.M., & Donnerstein, E., (Eds), *Pornography and Sexual Aggression,* "Sexual Signalling and Sexual Aggression in Adolescent Relationships" by J.D. Goodchilds & G.L. Zellman, Academic Press, Orlando, p.234-243, 1984.

Margolin, L., Craft, J.L., "Child Abuse by Adolescent Caregivers", *Journal of Family Violence,* V.114, No.3, p.365-373, 1990.

Margolin, L., "Group Therapy as a Means of Learning About the Sexually Assaultive Adolescent", *International Journal of Offender Therapy and Comparative and Comparative Criminology,* 25, p.45-54, 1981.

Margolin, L., "A Treatment Model for the Adolescent Sex Offender", *Journal of Offender Counselling Services and Rehabilitation,* 8, p.1-121983.

Markley, O., "A Study of Aggressive Sex Misbehavior in Adolescents Brought to Juvenile Court", *American Journal of Orthopsychiatry,* V.20, p.719-731, 1950.

Martin, J.E., Kourany, R.F.C., "Child Abuse by Adolescent Babysitters", *Child Abuse and Neglect,* 4, p.15-22, 1980.

Mathews, F. & Stermac, L., *Adolescent Sex Offenders: A Tracking Study,* Central Toronto Youth Services, Toronto, 1989.

Mathews, F., *Adolescent Sex Offenders: A Needs Study,* Central Toronto Youth Services, Toronto, 1987.

Mathias, R.A., (Ed), *Sourcebook for Treatment of the Violent Juvenile Offender,* "A Method for Treating the Adolescent Sex Offender" by S. Lane & P.A. Zamora, National Council on Crime and Delinquency, p.347-354, 1985.

McConaghy, N., Blaszczynsky, A., Armstrong, M., & Kidson, W., "Resistance to Treatment of Adolescent Sex Offenders", *Archives of Sexual Behaviour,* V.18, p.97-107, 1989.

McCraw, R.K., Pegg-McNab, J., "Rorschach Comparisons of Male Juvenile Sex Offenders and Non-sex Offenders", *Journal of Personality Assessment,* V.53, p.546-553, Fall 1989.

Monastersky, C., *Statistics on Sexual Offenders – Juvenile Sexual Offender Program,* University of Washington Adolescent Clinic, Seattle, Washington, 1985.

Monck, E., *"The Outcome of Treatment After Sexual Offending – Recent American Experiences with Juveniles",* A Paper given to Lamplugh Conference on the Sentencing of Sex Offenders, 1991.

O'Brien, M.J., *Characteristics of Male Adolescent Sibling Incest Offenders – Preliminary Findings,* The Safer Society Program, Orwell, 1989.

O'Brien, M. & Bera, W., "Adolescent Sexual Offenders: A Descriptive Typology", *Preventing Sexual Abuse,* V.1, No.3, p.1-4, 1986.

O'Brien, M., "Adolescent Sexual Offenders : A Community Faces Reality", *Change : A Juvenile Justice Quarterly,* Mimeo, 5, p.16-18,

O'Brien, M., "Adolescent Sexual Offenders : An Outpatient Program's Perspective on Research Directions", *Adolescent Sex Offenders: Issues in Research and Treatment,* Research Monograph, National Centre for the Prevention and Control of Rape, 1985.

Otey, E. & Ryan, G. (Eds), *Adolescent Sex Offenders, Issues in Research and Treatment,* "Recent Developments in the Treatment of Adolescent Sex Offenders" by F.H. Knopp, National Institute of Mental Health, Rockville, Maryland, DHHS Pub. No. (ADM) 85-1396, 1985.

Otey, E. & Ryan, G. (Eds), *Adolescent Sex Offenders, Issues in Research and Treatment,* "Methodological and Ethical Issues in Evaluating and Treating of Adolescent Sex Offenders" by J.V. Becker & G.A.G. Abel, National Institute of Mental Health, Rockville, Maryland, DHHS Pub. No. (ADM) 85-13960, p.109-129, 1985.

Pierce, L.H. & Pierce, R.L., "Incestuous Victimization by Juvenile Sex Offenders", *Journal of Family Violence,* V.2, No.4, p.351-364, Dec 1987.

Pomeroy, J.C., Behar, D. & Steward, M.A., "Abnormal Sexual Behaviour in Prepubescent Children", *British Journal of Psychiatry,* V.138, p.119-125, 1981.

Prinz, R. (Ed), *Advances in Behavioral Assessment of Children and Families,* "The Assessment of Adolescent Sexual Offenders" by J.V. Becker & M.S. Kaplan, JAI Press, Conni., 1989.

Reiss, A., Jr., "Sex Offences : The Marginal Status of the Adolescent", *Law and Contemporary Problems,* Duke University, School of Law, North Carolina, 1960.

Richardson, G., "Inadequate Intervention – The Need for Offence-specific Evaluation and Treatment to Effectively Deal with Young Offenders", *Social Work Today,* Dec 6, p.19-21, 1990.

Richardson, G., "Juvenile Sexual Perpetrators: A Model Approach and the Role of the Probation Service", *Probation Journal,* p.150-163, Dec 1990.

Richardson, J., Loss, P. & Ross, J.E., *Psychoeducational Curriculum for Adolescent Sex Offenders,* (Available from the Authors)1988.

Roberts, R.E., Abrams, L., and Finch, J.R., "Delinquent Sexual Behaviour Among Adolescents", *Medical Aspects of Human Sexuality,* V.7(1), p.162-175, 1973.

Ryan, G., "Victim to Victimiser", *Journal of Interpersonal Violence,* V.4, p.325-341, 1989.

Ryan, G., Lane, S., Davis, J. & Isaac, C., Juvenile Sex Offenders : Development and Correction, *Child Abuse & Neglect,* 11, p.385-395, 1987.

Ryan, G., "An Annotated Bibliography: Adolescent Perpetrators of Sexual Molestation of Children", *Child Abuse and Neglect,* V.10, p.125-132, 1986.

Ryan, G., Lane, S., Davis, J. & Isaac, C., "Juvenile Sex Offenders: Development and Correction", *Child Abuse & Neglect,* V.11, p.385-395, 1987.

Ryan, G., "Annotated Bibliography : Adolescent Perpetrators of Sexual Molestation of Children", *Child Abuse & Neglect,* 10, p.125-131, 1986.

Saunders, E., Awad, G.A. & White, G., "Male Adolescent Sexual Offender: The Offender and the Offence", Canadian Journal of Psychiatry, V.31, No.6, p.542-549, 1986.

Saunders, E.B. & Awad, G.A., "Assessment, Management and Treatment Planning for Male Adolescent Sex Offenders", *American Journal of Orthopsychiatry,* V.58(4), p.571-579, 1988.

Scavo, R.R., "Female Adolescent Sex Offenders: A Neglected Treatment Group", *Social Casework,* V.70, No.2, p.114-117, Feb 1989.

Sefarbi, R., "Admitters and Deniers Among Adolescent Sex Offenders and Their Families: A Preliminary Study", *American Journal of Orthopsychiatry,* V.60, 3, p.460-465, 1990.

Shorr, M., Speed, M. & Bartelt, C., "Syndrome of the Adolescent Child Molester", *American Journal of Psychiatry,* V.122, p.783-789, 1966.

Smele, A. & Cebula C., A Group Treatment Programme for Adolescent Sex Offenders : Five Steps Towards Resolution, *Child Abuse and Neglect,* V.11, No.2, p.247-254, 1987.

Smith, W.R., "Delinquency and Abuse Among Juvenile Sex Offenders", *Journal of Interpersonal Violence,* V.3, No.4, p.400-13, 1988.

Smith, W., & Monastersky, C., "Assessing Juvenile Sex Offenders' Risk for Re-offending", *Criminal Justice & Behavior,* V.13, p.115-140, 1986.

Smith, W., "Delinquency & Abuse Among Juvenile Sexual Offenders", *Journal of Interpersonal Violence,* V.3, No.4, p.400-413, 1988.

Smith, W.R., "Patterns of Re-offending among Juvenile Sex Offenders", Unpub. Manuscript, University of Washington, Juvenile Sex Offender Program, Seattle, Quoted in Davis, G.E. & Leitenberg, H. "Adolescent Sex Offenders" in Psychological Bulletin, V.101, p.417-427, 1987.1984.

Smith, H. & Israel, E., "Sibling Incest: A Study of the Dynamics of 25 Cases", *Child Abuse and Neglect,* V.11, p.101-108, 1987.

Smith, W.R. & Monastersky, C., "Assessing Juvenile Sexual Offenders Risk for Re-offending", *Criminal Justice & Behaviour,* 13, p.115-140, 1986.

Steen, C., *Treating Adolescent Sex Offenders in the Community,* Charles C Thomas, Springfield, Ill., 1989.

Stenson, P. & Anderson, C., "Treating Juvenile Sex Offenders and Preventing the Cycle of Abuse"*Journal of Child Care,* 3, p.91-102,1987.

Stermac, L. & Mathews, F., *Adolescent Sex Offenders: Towards a Profile,* Central Toronto Youth Services, Toronto, 1987.

Sullivan, T., "Turning a Blind Eye", *Youth in Society,* Central Toronto Youth Services, p.21, Jan 1986.

Tarter, R.E., Hegedus, A.M., Alterman, A.I. & Katz-Garris, L., "Cognitive Capacities of Juvenile Violent, Nonviolent, and Sexual Offenders", *Journal of Nervous and Mental Diseases,* V.171(9), p.564-567, 1983.

Terry, S., "Children Are Falling Victim to a New Kind of Sexual Offender– Other Children", *Rolling Stone,* p.67-72, October 31st, 1991.

Thomas, J.N., "Juvenile Sex Offenders : Physician and Parent Communication" *Paediatric Annals,* 9, p.161-170, 1984.

Thomas, J., "Juvenile Sexual Offenders: Guidelines For Assessment, *International Journal Offender Therapy, Comparative Criminology,* Child Abuse Victim Assistance Project, Research Foundation of Children's Hospital, Washington, DC, V.25, p.31-39.13, 1981.

Van Ness, S.R., "Rape as Instrumental Violence: A Study of Youth Offenders", *Journal of Offender Counselling Services and Rehabilitation,* 9, p.161-170, 1984.

Vinogradov, S., Dishotsky, N.I., Doty, A.K. & Tinklenberg, J.R., "Patterns of Behaviour in Adolescent Rape", *American Journal of Orthopsychiatry,* V.58(2), p.179-187, 1988.

Waggoner, R.W., "Juvenile Aberrant Sexual Behaviour", *American Journal of Orthopsychiatry,* 11, p.275-292, 1941.

Webberley, J., "Adolescent Sex Offenders", The Journal of Child Law, Frank Cass & Co, London, V.3, No.4, p.152-158, Sept-Dec 1991.

Wheeler, J. Robert, "Should Behavioral Interventions be Used in the Treatment of Adolescent Sex Offenders?", *Connections in the Prevention of Child Abuse,* V.1, No.1, p.6-8, 1986.

Wolpert Burgess, A. (Ed), *Sexual Assault Volume II,* "Adolescents and the Perceptions of Sexual Interaction Outcomes" by J Goodchilds, G Zellman, P. Johnson & R. Giarusso, Garland Publishing Company, N.Y., 1988.

Wyatt, G., & Powell, G., (Eds), *Lasting Effects of Child Sexual Abuse,* "The Effects of Child Sexual Abuse on Adolescent Sexual Offenders" by J. Becker, Sage, C.11, p.194-207, 1988.

Yates, A., "Children Eroticised by Incest", *Journal of the American Academy of Child and Adolescent Psychiatry,* V.27, p.254-257, 1982.

Part B

Abel, G., Cunningham-Rathner, J., Becker., J.V., & McHugh,J., *Motivating Sex Offenders for Treatment with Feedback of their Psychophysical Assessment,* Paper presented at the World Congress of Behaviour Therapy, Washington, DC, 1983.

Abel, G.G., Becker, J.V., Mittelman, M., Cunningham-Rathier, J., Rouleau, J. & Murphy, W., "Self Reported Sex Crimes in Non-incarcerated Paraphilias", *Journal of Interpersonal Violence,* V.2 (1), p.3-25, 1987.

Abel, G., Mittleman, M. & Becker, J., *Sex Offenders: Results of Assessment and Recommendations for Treatment,* 1985.

Abel, G., Barlow, D.H., Blanchard, E.B., & Guild. D., "The Components of Rapists' Sexual Arousal", *Archives of General Psychiatry,* V.34, p.895-903, 1977.

Abel, G., Becker, J., Cunningham-Rathner, J., Rouleau, J., Kaplan, M., and Reich, J., *The Treatment of Child Molesters: A Manual,* (Mimeo), SBC-TM, N.Y., 1984.

Abel, G., Becker, J., Cunningham-Rathner, J. & Lucas, L., *Recent Advancements in the Treatment of Sexually Violent Men,* 1983.

Adleson, J. (Ed), *Handbook of Adolescent Psychology,* "Strategic Interactions in Early Adolescence" by D. Elkind, Wiley & Son, N.Y., 1980.

American Humane Association (AHA), *National Study on Child Neglect and Abuse Reporting,* Denver, 1981.

Badgley, R., *Sexual Offences Against Children,* The Ministry of Justice, the Attorney General, and the Ministry of National Health and Welfare, Ottawa, 1984.

Bagley, C. & Ramsey, R., "Sexual Abuse in Childhood: Psychosocial Outcome and Implications for Social Work Practice", *Journal of Social Work and Human Sexuality,* V.4, p.33-37, 1985.

Baker, A.W. & Duncan, S.P., "Child Sexual Abuse : A Study of Prevalence in Great Britain", *Child Abuse and Neglect,* V.9, p.457-467, 1985.

Bays, K., & Freeman-Longo, R., *Why Did I Do It Again? Understanding My Cycle of Problem Behaviours,* The Safer Society Press, Shoreham Depot Road, RR1, Box 24-B Orwell, VT05760-9756, 1989.

Ben-Aron, M.H., Huckle, S.J., & Webster, C.D., (Eds), *Clinical Criminology: The Assessment and Treatment of Criminal Behaviour,* "Sex Offenders: Results of Assessment and Recommendations for Treatment", by G.G. Abel, M.S. Mittelman & J.V. Becker, M & M Graphic, Toronto, p.191-205, 1985.

Bentovim, A., Elton, A., Hildebrand, J., Tranter, M. & Vizard, E., *Child Sexual Abuse Within the Family : Assessment and Treatment,* Butterworth, London, 1988.

Bentovim, A., Elton, A., Hildebrand, J., Tranter, M. & Vizard, E. (Eds), *Child Sexual Abuse Within the Family : Assessment and Treatment,* "Understanding the Phenomenon of Sexual Abuse. A Family Systems View of Causation" by A. Bentovim, Butterworth, London, Ch.3, p.40-57, 1988.

Bentovim, A., Boston, P. & Van Elburg, A., "Child Sexual Abuse – Children and Families Referred to a Treatment Project and the Effects of Intervention", *British Medical Journal,* V.295, p.1453-1457, 1987.

Blair, C.D. & Lanyon, R.I., "Exhibitionism: Etiology and Treatment", *Psychological Bulletin*, V.89, p.439-463, 1981.

Bluglass, R., "Indecent Exposure in the West Midlands", *Sex Offenders in the Criminal Justice System*, Cropwood Conference Series No.12, University of Cambridge, Institute of Criminology, Cambridge, 1980.

Blumberg, M., "Psychology of the Abusing Parent", *American Journal of Psychotherapy*, V.28, p.21-29, 1974.

Brecher, E.M., *Treatment Programs for Sex Offenders*, U.S. Dept of Justice, Washington, DC, Jan 1978.

Briere, J., & Runtz, M., "University Males' Sexual Interest in Children: Predicting Potential Indices of "Paedophilia" in a Non-forensic Sample", *Child Abuse and Neglect*, V.13 p.65-75, 1989.

Briere, J., & Runtz, M., "Symptomatology Associated with Childhood Sexual Victimization in a Non-Clinical Adult Sample", *Child Abuse and Neglect*, V.12 p.51-59, 1989.

Brown, A. & Finkelhor, D., *Impact of Child Sexual Abuse: Review of Research*, Family Violence Research Program, Durham NC, 1985.

Burgess, A. & Holmstrom, L., "Rape: Sexual Disruption and Recovery", *American Journal of Orthopsychiatry*, V.49, p.648-657, 1978.

Burgess, A.W., Groth, N.A., Holmstrom, L.A., & Sgroi, S.M., *Sexual Assault of Children and Adolescents*, D.C. Heath, Toronto, 1978.

Butler, S., *Conspiracy of Silence: The Trauma of Incest*, New Glide Publications, San Francisco, 1978.

Butler Sloss, Lord Justice E., *Report of the Inquiry into Child Abuse in Cleveland*, HMSO, 1988.

Cautela, J.R. & Wisocki, P.A., "Covert Sensitisation for the Treatment of Sexual Deviation", *Psychological Record*, V.21, p.37-48, 1971.

Chasnoff, M.D., Burns, W.J., Schnoll, S.H., Burns, K., Chisum, G. & Kyle-Spore, L., "Maternal-neonatal Incest", *American Journal of Orthopsychiatry*, V.56, p.577-580, 1986.

Chatz, T.L., "Recognizing and Treating Dangerous Sex Offenders", *International Journal of Offender Therapy and Comparative Criminology*, V.16, No.2, p.109-115, 1972.

Chiswick, D., "Sex Crimes", *British Journal of Psychiatry*, V.143, p.236-241, 1983.

Christiansen, K., Ellers-Nielsen, M., Le Marine, L., & Sturup, G., "Recidivism Among Sex Offenders", *Scandinavian Studies in Criminology*, Tavistock, London, V.1, p.55-8, 1965.

Conte, J. & Shore, D. (Eds), *Social Work and Child Sexual Abuse*, "The Child Molester: Clinical Observations", Haworth, N.Y., 1982.

Conte, J., "The Effects of Sexual Abuse on Children, A Critique and Suggestions for Future Research", *Victimology*, V.10, p.110-130, 1985.

Conte, J.R., Schuerman, J., & Berliner, L., *The Behaviour of Sexually Abused Children at Intake and Twelve Months Later*, Unpublished manuscript available from the first Author,at 969 E.60th St., Chicago, IL 60637, 1989.

Conte, J.R., Wolf, S. & Smith, T., "What Sexual Offenders Tell us About Prevention Strategies", *Child Abuse and Neglect*, V.13(2), p.293-301, 1989.

Davis, G.E. & Leitenberg, H., "Adolescent Sex Offenders", *Psychological Bulletin*, V.101, p.417-427, 1987.

Dixson, A.R., "The Hormonal Control of Sexual Behaviour in Primates", *Oxford Review of Reproductive Biology*, V.5, p.131-219, 1983.

Eisenberg, N., Owens, R.G. & Dewey, M.E., "Attitudes of Health Professionals to Child Sexual Abuse and Incest", *Child Abuse and Neglect*, V.11 (1), p.109-116, 1987.

Evans, D.R., "Masturbatory Fantasy and Sexual Deviation", *Behaviour, Research and Therapy*, V.6, p.17-19, 1968.

Faller, K.C., *Understanding Child Sexual Maltreatment*, Sage, Beverley Hills, 1990.

Finkelhor, D., *Child Sexual Abuse: New Theory and Research*, "Four Preconditions: A Model", Free Press, N.Y., 1984.

Finkelhor, D. & Russell, D., *"Women as Perpetrators"*, 1984.

Finkelhor, D., *Sexually Victimised Children*, Free Press, N.Y., 1979.

Finkelhor, D., *A Source Book on Child Sexual Abuse*, "Initial and Long Term Effects: A Conceptual Framework" by D. Finkelhor & A. Browne, Sage, Beverley Hills, 1986.

Finkelhor, D. & Hotaling, G., "Sexual Abuse in a National Survey of Adult Men and Women: Prevalence, Characteristics & Risk Factors", *Child Abuse and Neglect*, V.14, No.1, p.19-28, 1990.

Finklehor, D., & Hotaling, G., *Sexual Abuse in the National Incidence Study of Child Abuse and Neglect*, Report to National Centre on Child Abuse and Neglect, 1983.

Finklehor, D. (Ed), *A Sourcebook on Child Sexual Abuse*, "Prevalence" by S.D. Peters, G.E. Wyatt & D. Finklehor, Sage, p.15-59, 1986.

Finklehor, D. (Ed), *A Sourcebook on Child Sexual Abuse*, "Abusers: Special Topics" by D. Finklehor, Sage, p.119-242, 1986.

Finklehor, D., *Sexually Victimized Children*, "Older Partners", Free Press, N.Y., p.74, 1979.

Fitch, J.H., "Men Convicted of Sexual Offences Against Children: A Descriptive Follow-up Study", *British Journal of Criminology*, V.3 (1), p.18-37, 1962.

Forward, S. & Buck, C., *Betrayal of Innocence: Incest and its Devastation*, J.P. Tarcher, Los Angeles, 1978.

Freeman-Longo, R., "The Impact of Sexual Victimisation on Males", *Child Abuse and Neglect*, V.10, p.411-14, 1986.

Fritz, G.S., Stoll, K. & Wagner, N., "A Comparison of Males and Females Who Were Molested as Children", *Journal of Sex and Marital Therapy*, V.7, p.54-59, 1981.

Fromuth, M. & Burkhart, B., "Long-term Psychological Correlates of Childhood Sexual Abuse in Two Samples of College Men", *Child Abuse and Neglect*, V.13, No.4, p.533-542, 1989.

Fromuth, M. & Burkhart, B., "Childhood Sexual Victimization Among College Men: Definitional and Methodological Issues", *Violence and Victims*, V.2, No.4, p.241-253, 1987.

Furniss, T., "Mutual Influence and Inter-locking Professional-Family Process in the Treatment of Child Sexual Abuse and Incest", *Child Abuse and Neglect*, V.7(2), p.207-223, 1983.

Furniss, T., "Family Process in the Treatment of Intrafamilial Sexual Abuse", *Journal of Family Therapy*, V.5 (4), p.263-278, 1983.

Gebhard, P.H., Gagnon, J.H., Pomeroy, W.B., & Christiansen, C.V., *Sex Offenders: An Analysis of Types*, Harper & Row, N.Y., 1965.

Gibbens, T.C.W., Soothill, K.I. and Way, C.K., "Sibling and Parent-Child Incest Offenders: A Long Term Follow-up", *British Journal of Criminology*, V.18 (1), p.40-52, 1978.

Gil, D.G., *Violence Against Children: Physical Abuse in the United States*, Harvard University Press, Cambridge, MA, 1970.

Gittleson, N.L., Eacott, S.E. & Mehta, B.M., "Victims of Indecent Exposure", *British Journal of Psychiatry*, V.132, p.61-66, 1978.

Glasgow, D.V. & Bentall, R.P., "What do Expert Witnesses in Child Sexual Abuse Think They Are Doing? - 'Diagnosis', and the Sexually Accurate Doll 'Test' as Professional Myths", *The Liverpool Law Review*, V.XI(1), p.45-57, 1989.

Gomes-Schwartz, B., *Sexually Exploited Children: Service and Research Project*, "Juvenile Sexual Offenders", US Dept of JusticeWashington, D.C., 1984.

Good, J., *Coping with Incest*, The Vermont Vanguard Press, No.4, p.10-11, March 6-13, 1981.

Gorry, P.J., Incest: The Offence and Police Investigation, Unpub. M Phil Thesis in Criminology, University of Cambridge, 1986.

Greer, J. & Stuart, I. (Eds), *The Sexual Aggressor: Current Perspectives on Treatment*, "Treatment and Evaluation Issues with the Mentally Retarded Sex Offender", by W.D. Murphy, E.M. Coleman & M.R. Haynes, Van Nostrand Reinhold, N.Y., 1983.

Groth, A.N. & Freeman-Longo, R., *Men Who Rape: The Psychology of the Offender*, Plenum, N.Y., 1979.

Groth, N. & Burgess, A., "Sexual Trauma in the Life Histories of Rapists and Child Molesters", *Victimology: An International Journal*, V.4, p.10-16, 1979.

Groth, N.A., & Birnbaum, J., "Adult Sexual Orientation and the Attraction to Underage Persons", *Archives of Sexual Behaviour*, V.7, p.175-181, 1978.

Groth, A., Longo, R. & McFadin, B., "Undetected Recidivism Among Rapists and Child Molesters", *Crime and Delinquency*, V.28, p.102-106, 1982.

Hall, G.C.N., Proctor, W.C. & Nelson, G.M., "Validity of Physiological Measures of Paedophiliac Sexual Arousal in a Sex Offender Population", *Journal of Consulting and Clinical Psychology*, V.56, p.118-122, 1988.

Hammer, E.F. & Glueck, B.C., "Psychodynamic Patterns in Sex Offence: A Four-Factor Theory", *Psychiatric Quarterly*, V.3, p.325-345, 1957.

Haugaard, J. & Emery, R., "Methodological Issues in Child Sexual Abuse Research", *Child Abuse and Neglect*, V.13, p.89-100, 1989.

Haugaard, J. & Dickon Reppucci, N., *The Sexual Abuse of Children*, Josey-Bass, San Francisco, 1988.

Hayes, S., Brownell, K. & Barlow, D., "Heterosexual Skills Training and Covert Sensitisation. Effects on Social Skills and Sexual Arousal in Sexual Deviants", *Behaviour Research and Therapy*, V.21, p.383-392, 1983.

Helfer, R., & Kemp, C.H. (Eds), *Child Abuse and Neglect: The Family in the Community*, "Sexual Exploitation" by M.D. Schecter, & L. Roberge, Ballinger, Cambridge, Mass, 1976.

Helfer, R., ,"The Etiology of Child Abuse", *Paediatrics*, V.15, p.779-824, 1973.

Herman, J., *Father-Daughter Incest*, Harvard Univ. Press, Cambridge, Mass, 1981.

Hibbard, R., Roghmann, K. & Hoekelman, R., "Genitalia in Children's Drawings: An Association with Sexual Abuse", *Paediatrics*, V.79, p.129-137, 1987.

Holder, W. (Ed), *Sexual Abuse of Children Denver, Colorado*, "The Nature and Extent of Child Abuse in Contemporary American Society" by L. Browne & W. Holder, American Humane Association, Denver, Colorado, 1980.

Hollin, C.R., & Howells, K., (Eds), *Clinical Approaches to Sex Offenders and Their Victims*, "Clinical Work with Families in Which Sexual Abuse has Occurred" by A. Bentovim., John Wiley & Sons, Ch.8, p.179-208, 1991.

Hollin, C.R., & Howells, K., (Eds), *Clinical Approaches to Sex Offenders and Their Victims*, "Assessment of Adult Sexual Interest" by W.D. Murphy, M.R. Haynes, John Wiley & Sons, p.77-92, 1991.

Horton, A.L., Johnson, B.L., Roundy, L.M. & Williams, D. (Eds), *The Incest Perpetrator: A Family Member No-one Wants to Treat*, "Adolescent/Sibling Incest Perpetrators" by L.H. Pierce & R.L. Pierce, Sage, California, 1990.

Jones, D.P.H., "Individual Psychotherapy for the Sexually Abused Child", *Child Abuse and Neglect: The International Journal*, V.10, p.377-385, 1986.

Justice, B. & Justice, R., *The Broken Taboo: Sex in the Family*, Human Science Press, N.Y., 1979.

Karpman, B., *The Sex Offender and his Offences, Etiology, Pathology, Psychodynamics and Treatment*, JulianN.Y., 1954.

Katz, S. & Mazur, M., *Understanding the Rape Victim: A Synthesis of Research Findings*, John Wiley, N.Y., 1979.

Kelly, L., *Surviving Sexual Violence*, Polity Press, Cambridge, 1988.

Kelly, L., "Unspeakable Acts: Violence by and Between Women", *Trouble and Strife*, V.21, 1991.

Kempe, C.H. & Helfer, R.E. (Eds), *The Battered Child*, "A Psychiatric Study of Parents Who Abuse Infants and Small Children" by B.F. Steel & C.D. Pollack, University of Chicago Press, Chicago, 1968.

Kempe, C.H., "Recent Developments in the Field of Child Abuse", *Child Abuse and Neglect*, V.3, ix-xv, 1979.

Knopp, F.H., *Retraining Adult Sex Offenders : Methods and Models*, Safer Society Press, N.Y., 1984.

Knopp, F.H. & Lackey, L.B., *Sex Offenders identified as Intellectually Disabled : A Summary of Data from 40 Treatment Providers*, Safer Society Program, Orwell, VT 05760-9756, 1987.

Kolarsky, A. & Madlafousek, J., "The Inverse Role of Preparatory Erotic Stimulation in Exhibitionists; Phalometric Studies", *Archives of Sexual Behaviour*, V.12, p.123-148, 1983.

Kremsdorf, R.B., Holmen, M.L. & Laws, D.R., "Orgasmic Reconditioning Without Deviant Imagery; A Case Report with a Paedophile", *Behaviour Research and Therapy*, V.18, p.203-207, 1980.

La Fontaine, J.S., *A Sociological Study of Cases of Child Sexual Abuse in Britain*, ESRC end of award report no. G0023 2244, 1987.

La Fontaine, J., *Child Sexual Abuse*, An ESRC Research Briefing, ESRC, Swindon, 1988.

Langevin, R., Paitich, D., Ramsay, G., Anderson, C., Kamrad, J., Pope, s., Geller, G., Pearl, L. & Newman, S., "Experimental Studies of the Etiology of Genital Exhibitionism", *Archives of Sexual Behaviour*, V.8, p.307-331, 1979.

Langevin, R. (Ed), *Erotic Preference, Gender Identity and Aggression*, "Are Incestuous Fathers Paedophiliac and Aggressive?" by R. Langevin, L. Handy, Hook, Day & A. Russon, Erlbaum, N.Y., 1985.

Laufer, M., "The Central Masturbation Fantasy, The Final Sexual Organisation and Adolescence", *Psychoanalytic Study of the Child*, V.31, p.297-316, 1976.

Laws, D.R. & O'Neil, J.A., "Variations on Masturbatory Conditioning", *Behavioural Psychotherapy*, V.9, p.111-136, 1981.

Laws, D. (Ed), *Relapse Prevention with Sex Offenders*, Guilford, N.Y., 1989.

Lester, D., "Incest", *Journal of Sex Research*, V.8, p.268-285, 1972.

Lokianowicz, N., "Incest II: Other Types of Incest", *British Journal of Psychiatry*, V.120, p.308-313, 1972.

Lukianowicz, N., "Incest 1 – Paternal incest: 2 – Other Types of Incest", *British Journal of Psychiatry*, V.120, p.301-13, 1972.

MacDonald, J.M., *Rape Offenders and Their Victims*, Charles C Thomas, Springfield, IL., 1971.

Margolin, L., Craft, J.L., *"Child Sexual Abuse by Caretakers"*, Presented at the Changing Family Conference XVIII:Health Issues and Families, Iowa City, Iowa, Feb 1989.

Marshall, W.L., Barbaree, H.E., & Christopher, D., "Sex Offenders Against Female Children: Sexual Preferences for Age of Victim and Type of Behaviour", *Canadian Journal of Behavioural Science*, V.18, p.424-439, 1986.

Marshall, W.L., Laws, D.R. & Barbaree, H.E. (Eds), *Handbook of Sexual Assault: Issues, Theories and Treatment of the Offender*, "A Conditioning Theory of the Etiology and Maintenance of Deviant Sexual Preference and Behaviour", Plenum, N.Y., 1990.

McClintock, F.H., "Criminal Careers of Sex Offenders: Recidivism, Criminal Justice and Politics", *Sex Offenders in the Criminal Justice System*, Cropwood Conference Series No.12, University of Cambridge Institute of Criminology, Cambridge, 1980.

McGuire, R.J., Carlisle, J.M. & Young, B.G., "Sexual Deviations as Conditioned Behaviour; a Hypothesis", *Behaviour, Research and Therapy*, V.2, p.185-190, 1965.

McLeer, S.V., Deblinger, E., Atkins, M.S., Foa, E.B. & Ralphe, D.L., "Post-traumatic Stress Disorder in Sexually Abused Children", *Journal of the American Academy of Child and Adolescent Psychiatry*, V.27, p.650-654, 1988.

Meiselman, D., *Incest: A Psychological Study of Causes and Effects with Treatment Recommendations*, Jossey-Bass, San Francisco, 1978.

Melnick B. & Hurley, J.R., "Distinctive Personality Attributes of Child-abusing Mothers", *Journal of Consulting and Clinical Psychology*, V.33, p.746-749, 1969.

Meyer, L. & Romero, J., *Ten Year Follow-up of Sex Offender Recidivism*, Joseph Peters Institute (112 S.16th St.), Philadelphia, 1980.

Mezey, G., Vizard, E., Hawkes, C., & Austin, R., "A Community Treatment Programme for Convicted Sex Offenders: A Preliminary Report", *The Journal of Forensic Psychiatry*, V.2, No.1, p.11-25, 1991.

Mohr, J.W., Turner, R.E. & Jerry, M.B., *Paedophilia and Exhibitionism: A Handbook*, University of Toronto Press, Toronto, 1964.

Morgan, R., *Going Too Far: The Personal Chronicle of a Feminist*, Vintage Books, N.Y., 1978.

Mrazek, P.B., Kempe, C.H., (Eds) *Sexually Abused Children and Their Families*, "Recognition of Child Sexual Abuse in the United Kingdom" by P.B. Mrazek, M. Lynch & A. Bentovim, Pergamon Press, Oxford, 1981.

Mrazek, P.B., Kempe, C.H., (Eds) *Sexually Abused Children and Their Families*, "A Comprehensive Child Sexual Abuse Treatment Program" by H. Giarretto, Pergamon Press, Oxford, p.179-198, 1981.

Mrazek, P.B., Kemp, C.H., (Eds) *Sexually Abused Children and Their Families*, "The Effects of Child Sexual Abuse: Methodological Considerations" by P.B. Mrazek, Pergamon Press, Oxford, 1981.

Myer, L. & Romero, J., *A Ten Year Follow-up Of Sex Offender Recidivism*, Joseph J. Peters Institute, Philadelphia, PA, 1980.

Nadelson, C. Et Al., "A Follow-up Study of Rape Victims", *American Journal of Psychiatry*, V.139, p.1266-1270, 1982.

NCCAN, *Study of National Incidence and Prevalence of Child Abuse and Neglect*, U.S. Department of Health and Human Services, 1988.

Oates, M.R., "A Classification of Child Abuse and Its Relation to Treatment and Prognosis", *Child Abuse and Neglect*, V.3, p.907-915, 1979.

Peters, J.J., "Children Who Are Victims of Sexual Assault and the Psychology of Offenders", *American Journal of Psychotherapy*, V.30, p.398-412, 1976.

Prins, H.A., *Offenders, Deviants or Patients?*, Tavistock, London, 1980.

Pynoos, R.S. & Eth, S., *"Post-traumatic Stress Disorder in Children"*, American Psychiatric Association, Los Angeles, 1985.

Quinsey, V.L. & Chaplin, T., "Penile Responses of Child Molesters and Normals to Descriptions of Encounters with Children Involving Sex and Violence", *Journal of Interpersonal Violence*, V.3, p.259-74, 1988.,

Radzinowicz, L., *Sexual Offences; A Report of the Cambridge Dept of Criminal Science*, McMillan, London, 1957.

Risin, L. & Koss, M., "The Sexual Abuse of Boys: Prevalence and Descriptive Characteristics of Childhood Victimizations", *Journal of Interpersonal Violence*, V.2, No.3, p.309-323, 1987.

Robins, L.W., "Sturdy Childhood Predictors of Adult Anti-Social Behavior: Replications from Longitudinal Studies", *Psychological Medicine*, V.8, p.611-622, 1978.

Rooth, F.G., "Indecent Exposure and Exhibitionism", *British Journal of Hospital Medicine*, V.5, p.521-533, 1971.

Rooth, F.G., "Exhibitionism: An Eclectic Approach to its Management", *British Journal of Hospital Medicine*, V.23, p.366-370, 1980.

Rooth, G., "Exhibitionism, Sexual Violence and Paedophilia", *British Journal of Psychiatry*, V.122, p.705-710, 1973.

Rosen, I., (Ed), *Sexual Deviation*, "Some Aspects of the Role of Aggression in the Perversions" by M. Glasser, Oxford University Press, Oxford, p.278-305, 1978.

Rosenfeld, A.A., Bailey, R., Siegel, B. & Bailey, G., "Determining Incestuous Contact Between Parent and Child: Frequency of Child Touching Parents' Genitals in a Non-clinical Population", *Journal of the American Academy of Child Psychiatry*, V.25, p.481-484, 1986.

Rosenfeld, A.A., Siegel, B. & Bailey, G., "Familial Bathing Patterns: Implications for Cases of Alleged Molestation and for Paediatric Practice", *Paediatrics*, V.79, p.224-229, 1987.

Ross, J.E., *Correctional Sex Offender Treatment Program Guidelines*, Jonathan E. Ross, M.A., Inc., 1990.

Ruch, F., *Best Kept Secret: Sexual Abuse of Children*, Prentice-Hall, Englewood Cliffs, N.J., 1980.

Russell, D., "The Incidence and Prevalence of Intrafamilial and Extra Familial Sexual Abuse on Female Children", *Child Abuse and Neglect*, V.7, p.133-146, 1983.

Russell, D.E.H., *Sexual Exploitation*, Sage,California1984.

Russell, D.E.H., *Sexual Exploitation: Rape, Child Sexual Abuse and Workplace Harassment*, Sage, 1984.

Russell, D., *The Secret Trauma: Incest in the Lives of Girls and Women*, Basic Books, N.Y., 1984.

Salter, A.C., *Treating Child Sex Offenders & Victims*, "Sexual Cognition Scale" by G.G. Abel & J.V. Becker (1985), Sage, California, 1988.

Salter, A.C., *Treating Child Sex Offenders and Victims – A Practical Guide*, "Relapse Prevention. A Method of Enhancing Maintenance of Change in Sex Offenders" by W.D. Pithers, K.M. Kashima, G.F., Cumming & L.S. Beal, Sage Pub. Inc., p.131-170, 1988.

Sanford, L., *The Silent Children: A Parents' Guide to the Prevention of Child Sexual Abuse*, Doubleday Anchor Press, N.Y., 1980.

Seghorn, T., Prentky, R., & Boucher, R., *Childhood Sexual Abuse in the Lives of Sexually Aggressive Offenders*, 1987.

Seigel, J., Sorenson, S., Golding, J., Burnam, A. & Stein, J., "The Prevalence of Childhood Sexual Assault: The Los Angeles Epidemiologic Area Project", *American Journal of Epidemiology*, V.1266, p.1141-1153, 1987.

Sgroi, S.M. (Ed), *Handbook of Clinical Intervention in Child Sexual Abuse*, "Sibling Incest" by C. Laredo, Heath and Co., Lexington, Mass., p.177-188, 1982.

Shorkey, C.T., "Psychological Characteristics of Child Abusers: Speculation and Need for Research", *Child Abuse and Neglect*, V.2, p.69-76, 1978.

Silberman, G. & Silberman, L. *Case History: Phobic Avoidance of Sex*, Unpublished ms., 1981.

Smith, M. & Grocke, M., *Normal Family Sexuality and Sexual Knowledge in Children*, (In preparation), 1990.

Snaith, P., "Exhibitionism, A Clinical Conundrum", *British Journal of Psychiatry*, V.143, p.231-235, 1983.

Stevenson, J. & Jones, I.H., "Behaviour Therapy Techniques for Exhibitionism", *Archives of General Psychiatry*, V.27, p.239-241, 1972.

Stewart, I.R. & Green, J.C. (Eds), *Victims of Sexual Aggression: Treatment of Children, Women and Men*, "Group Work with Pre-adolescent Sexual Abuse Victims" by L. Berliner, & E. Ernst, Van Nostrand Reinhold, N.Y., 1984.

Straus, M., Gelles, R. & Steinmetz, S., *Behind Closed Doors: Violence in the American Family*, Doubleday, N.Y., 1979.

Summit, R.C. & Kryso, J., "Sexual Abuse of Children: A Clinical Spectrum", *American Journal of Orthopsychiatry*, V.48, p.237-251, 1978.

Trepper, T.S. & Barrett, M.J., *Treating Incest: A Multiple Systems Perspective*, The Haworth Press, 1986.

Tufts New England Medical Centre, *"Sexually Exploited Children: Services and Research Project"*, (Final Report for the Office of Juvenile Justice and Delinquency Prevention), Washington DC, U.S. Dept of Justice, 1984.

Van Scoyk, S., Gray, J., Jones, D.P.H., "A Theoretical Framework for Evaluation and Treatment of the Victims of Child Sexual Assault by a Nonfamily Member", *Family Process*, V.27, p.105-112, March 1988.

Walker, L., (Ed), *Handbook on Sexual Abuse in Children*, "The Impact of Sexual Abuse in Children: Empirical Findings" by J Conte & L Berliner, In press,

Warshaw, R., *I Never Called it Rape: The Ms. Report on Recognizing, Fighting and Surviving Date and Acquaintance Rape*, Harper and Row, N.Y., 1988.

Watson, J.W., Switzer, R.E. & Hirschberg, J.C., *My Friend, the Babysitter*, Golden Press, N.Y., 1971.

Weeks, R., "The Sexually Exploited Child", *Southern Medical Journal*, V.69, No.7, p.848-850, 1976.

West, D.J. (Ed), *Sexual Victimization*, "Sexual Molestation of Young Girls: A Retrospective Study" by C.L. Nash and D.J. West, Gower, Aldershot, 1985.

Wyatt, G., & Powell, G., (Eds), *Lasting Effects of Child Sexual Abuse*, "Behaviour Problems in Sexually Abused Children: An Adaptational Perspective" by J. Becker, Sage, Beverley Hills, 1988.

Wyatt, G., & Powell, G., (Eds), *Lasting Effects of Child Sexual Abuse*, "Post Sexual Abuse Trauma" by J. Briere, & M. Runtz, Sage, Beverley Hills,

Wyatt, G., "The Sexual Abuse of Afro-American and White American Women in Childhood", *Child Abuse and Neglect*, V.9, p.507-519, 1985.

Wyatt, G.E. & Peters, D.S., "Issues in the Definition of Child Sexual Abuse in Prevalence Research", *Child Abuse and Neglect*, V.10, p.231-240, 1986.

Wyre, R., "Sex Offenders and Their Rehabilitation", *Social Work Today*, V.18, p.10-11, 1987.

Wyre, R., *Working with Sex Offenders*, Gracewell Clinic, 1989.

Yurokoglu, A. & Kemph, J.P., "Children Not Severely Damaged by Incest With the Parent", *Journal of the American Academy of Child Psychiatry*, V.5, p.111-124, 1966.

Zalba, S.R., "The Abused Child: A Typology for Classification and Treatment", *Social Work*, V.12, p.70-79, 1967.

Part C

Ault, R. (Ed), *Developmental Perspectives*, "The Development of Prosocial Behavior and Moral Judgement" by D.M. Gelfand & D.P. Hartmann, Goodyear, Santa Monica, CA, p.216-266, 1980.

Bancroft, J., *Human Sexuality and Its Problems*, Churchill, Livingstone, Edinburgh, 1983.

Bandura, A., *Aggression: A Social Learning Analysis*, Prentice Hall, Englewood Cliffs, N.J., 1973.

Bellack, A.S., & Hersen, M. (Eds), *Handbook of Family Violence*, "Incest" by J.V. Becker & E.M. Coleman, Plenum, N.Y., 1988.

Berne, E., *Games People Play*, Penguin, London, 1964.

Buss, A.H. & Durkee, A. "An Inventory for Assessing Different Kinds of Hostility", *Journal of Consulting Psychology*, V.21, p.343-349, 1957.

Byng-Hall, J., "Family Myths Used as Defenses in Conjoint Family Therapy", *British Journal of Medical Psychology*, V.46, p.239-250, 1973.

Cook, M. & Wilson, G. (Eds), *Love and Attraction; An International Conference*, "Tactical Self-presentation and Interpersonal Attraction" by C.R. Figley, Pergamon, Oxford, 1979.

Eisenhower, M.S., *To Establish Justice, To Insure Domestic Tranquillity*, Final Report of the National Commission on Causes and Prevention of Violence, US Government Printing Office, Washington DC, 1969.

Emler, N., "Differential Involvement in Delinquency: Toward an Interpretation in Terms of Reputation Management", *Progress in Experimental Personality Research*, Academic Press, London, V.13, 1984.

Erikson, E.H., *Identity, Youth and Crisis*, Norton, N.Y., 1968.

Erikson, E.H., *Childhood and Society*, Norton, N.Y., 1950.

Evans, J., *Adolescent and Pre-adolescent Psychiatry*, Academic Press, London, 1982.

Ferreira, A.J., "Family Myths: The Covert Rules of the Relationship", *Confinia Psychiatry*, V.8, p.15-20, 1965.

Ferreira, A.J., "Family Myth and Homeostasis", *Archives of General Psychiatry*, V.9, p.457-463, 1963.

Francoeur, R., *Becoming a Sexual Person*, John Wiley and Sons, N.Y., 1982.

Freeman-Longo, R., & Bays, L., *Who Am I and Why Am I in Treatment?, A Guided Workbook for Clients in Evaluation and Beginning Treatment*, The Safer Society Press, Shoreham Depot Road RR1, Box 24-B, VT 05760-9756,

Freund, K., Scher, H. & Hucker, S., "The 'courtship' disorders", *Archives of Sexual Behaviour*, V.12, p.369-380, 1983.

Goffman, E., *Strategic Interaction*, Blackwell, Oxford, 1970.

Greer, R. & Donnerstein, E. (Eds), *Aggression: Theoretical and Empirical Review*, "Arousal and Aggressions" by D. Zillman, Academic Press, N.Y., 1983.

Grubin, D., & Gunn, J., *"The Imprisoned Rapist and Rape"*, Unpub. manuscript, based on a review of convicted rapists in England and Wales, Institute of Psychiatry, London, 1990.

Gurman, A. & Kniskern, D., (Eds), *Handbook of Family Therapy*, "Focal Family Therapy" by A. Bentovim, & H. Ratner, Basic Books, N.Y., 1990.

Harre, R. & Secord, P.F., *The Explanation of Social Behaviour*, Blackwell, Oxford, 1972.

Henggeler, S., *Delinquency in Adolescence*, Sage, 1989.

Hoffman, M.L., "Developmental Synthesis of Affect and Cognition and Its Implications for Altruistic Motivation", *Developmental Psychology*, V.11, p.607-622, 1975.

Home Secretary's Speech, "Review of Prison Treatment Facilities for Sex Offenders", The Lamplugh Conference on the Sentencing of Sex Offenders, 7 June 1991.

Kahn, T.J., *Pathways: A Guided Workbook for Youth Beginning Treatment*, Safer Society Press, Orwell, Vermont, 1990.

Katzenbach, N., *The Challenge of Crime in a Free Society*, Report by the President's Commission on Law Enforcement and the Administration of Justice, US Government Printing Office, Washington DC, 1976.

Knoth, R., Boyd, K. & Singer, B., "Empirical Tests of Sexual Selection Theory: Predictions in Onset, Intensity and Time Course of Sexual Arousal", *Journal of Sex Research*, V.24, p.73-89, 1988.

Limentani, A., "Perversions: Treatable and Untreatable", The 10th Glover Lecture, 10th November 1986, *Contemporary Psychoanalysis*, London, V.23, No.3, 1987.

Lloyd, & Walmsley, *Changes in Rape Offences, Sentencing*, Home Office Research Report, HMSO, London, 105,

MacLeod, M. & Saraga, E., "Challenging the Orthodoxy: Towards a Feminist Theory and Practice", *Feminist Review*, Issue 28, p.16-55,1988.

McDougall, J., "Identification, Neo-needs and Neo-Sexuality", *International Journal of Psychoanalysis*, V.67, p.19-31, 1986.

McGuire, R.J. and Vallance, M., "Aversion Therapy by Electric Shock; A Simple Technique", *British Medical Journal*, V.1, p.151-153, 1964.

Nowicki, S. & Strickland, B.R., "A Locus of Control Scale for Children", *Journal of Consulting and Clinical Psychology*, V.40, p.148-155, 1973.

Piers, E. & Harris, D.B., *The Piers-Harris Children's Self-Concept Scale*, Western Psychological Services, Los Angeles, 1983.

Platt, J.J., Spivack, G., Altman, N., Altman, D.S. & Peizer, S.B., "Adolescent Problem-solving Thinking", *Journal Consultant and Clinical Psychology*, V.42, p.787-793, 1974.

Rogozin, A., Basham, R., Crnic, K., Greenberg, M. & Robinson, N., "Effects of Maternal Age on Parenting Role", *Development Psychology*, V.18, p.627-634, 1982.

Ryan, G., Davis, J., Miyoshi, T., Lane, S. & Wilson, K., "Getting at the Facts: The First Report From the Uniform Data Collection System", *Interchange*, June, p.5-7, 1987.

Spence, S.H., "Teaching Social Skills to Children", *Journal Child Psychology and Psychiatry*, V.24, p.621-628, 1983.

Staub, C.T., *Positive Social Behaviour and Morality: Socialization and Development (Vol.2)*, Academic Press, N.Y., 1979.

Staub, C.T., "Instigation to Goodness: The Role of Social Norms and Interpersonal Influence", *Journal of Social Issues*, V.28, p.131-150, 1972.

Stoller, R.J., *Perversion, the Erotic Form of Hatred*, Harvester Press, 1976.

Strong, B. & Reynolds, R., *Understanding Our Sexuality*, West Publ. Co., St. Paul, Minn., 1982.

Summary Report of Denver Medical Society Task Force on Victims of Violence 1983-84, "Chairman, President's Task Force on Victims of Crime", Denver Medical Society, Denver CO, 1985.

Terr, L., "Life Attitudes, Dreams and Psychic Trauma in a Group of "Normal Children", *Journal of the American Association of Child Psychiatry*, V.22, p.221-230, 1983.

Terr, L., "Chowchilla Revisited: The Effects of Psychic Trauma Four Years After a School Bus Kidnapping", *American Journal of Psychiatry*, V.140, p.1543-1550, 1983.

Twentyman, C.T., & McFall, M., "Behavioural Training of Social Skills in Shy Males", *Journal of Consulting and Clinical Psychology*, V.43, p.384-395, 1975.

Vondura, J.I., "A Consideration of Caregiver Age Variables in Day-Care Settings", *Child Care Quarterly*, V.13, p.102-113, 1984.

Welldon, E.V., *Mother, Madonna, Whore: Idealisation and Denigration of Motherhood*, Free Association Books, 1988.

Wilson, G., *"The Secrets of Sexual Fantasy"*, London, 1978.

Zarbatany, L., Hartmann, D.P. & Gelfand, D.M., "Why Does Children's Generosity Increase with Age: Susceptibility to Experimenter Influence or Altruism", *Child Development*, V.56, p.746-756, 1985.

List of Contributors

Our thanks are due to the following people who contributed, in various ways, to the work of the Committee:

Gill Ackerley	Moreland Drive Children's Home
Steve Armstrong	Adolescent Sexual Abuse Offenders Counsellor
David Asher	Bradford Family Services Unit
Sylvia Aston	Detective Inspector, West Midlands Police
Margaret Austin	Strathclyde Regional Council
Dr A Bagadi	Dept of Child & Family Psychiatry
Susan Bailey	The Gardener Unit
Lesley Baker	Probation
Paul Baker	ACPO, NE London Probation Service
Colin Baldwin	NCH
Philip Batt	N Yorkshire Social Services Dept
Kathy Beale	Derbyshire Social Services
Jack Bebb	Juvenile Justice Centre
Adrian Bell	Child Protection Team Dudley Social Services
Sue Bell	Clinical Nurse, Specialist Child & Family Psychiatry Unit
Nigel Bennett	Barnardo's
R J Blackman	Downshead Children's Home
Pat Blackshaw	Child Protection, Hampshire Social Services
David Bliss	North Yorkshire Social Services
Stuart Bond	Scottish Office Education Dept
Jane Booth	P O Child Protection, Calderdale Social Services
Nadine Boole	Worksop College Boarding School
Lou Brindley	Archway I T Centre
Dr J Brock	Darlington Health Authority
Stewart Brodie	Tayside Regional Council
Dr D R Brook	JP, Magistrates Association
Alix Brown	Shropshire Social Services
Syntika Browne	Brent Social Services
Bettina Brunnen	Sydney House Communities
K Budd	The Oaks Centre
Felicity Budgen	Surrey Social Services
T J Burns	Gloucester Social Services
Sheila Burton	Polytechnic North London
Alice Butcher	Leicester Social Services
Walter Camplin	St Charles Youth Treatment Centre
Agapi Candilak	University of Bradford
Vera Carroll	Brookside Family Consultation Clinic
Roger Carruthers	Adolescent Services Manager, LB Redbridge Social Services
Alan Caygill	Bradford Social Services
Dr G Chew	West Surrey/NE Hants DHA
J Christopherson	Dept of Social Work, Nottingham University
Mary Claderhead	ChildLine, Scotland
Hedy Cleaver	Dartington Social Research Unit
Jim Clewlow	Clermont Child Protection Unit
Catherine Cohen	Magistrates Association
J S Cooksey	Brookside Family Centre
Bryan Cornick	NSPCC
Geoff Cooper	Detective Inspector, New Scotland Yard
Andrew Copp	Juvenile Justice Manager, Liverpool Social Services
Dianne Core	Childwatch
Sharon Cox	Devon Social Services Dept
K Crane	Det Chief Inspector, West Mercia Constabulary
H Croucher	The Oaks Centre
Celia Crowe	The Norfolk Agency
Peter Crowley	Clinical Psychologist, Winchester Health Authority
Dr E Crutchley	West Surrey/NE Hants DHA
Gerry Cullinan	Milton Keynes Health Authority
Pamela Dansell	Hammersmith & Fulham Social Services

Dr A K Darwish	Consultant Child Psychiatrist, Mid Glamorgan Health Authority
Jo Davenport	Sheffield Family & Community Services
Joanne Davies	Caldecott Community
Geoff Debelle	Centre for Community Health
Harriet Dempster	Dundee Social Services
Carol Dey	NSPCC, C S A Consultancy
Jennifer Disley	Blackburn & District Children's Homes
R W Dixon	DCI, Herts Police
Dr R Dobash	Dept of Sociology, Stirling University
Kevin Donohue	Child Protection, Hampshire Social Services
Anne Douglas	Young Peoples Unit
Betty Duffy	Strathclyde Regional Council
Mary Dundon	Lincolnshire Social Services
Dr K N Dwivedi	Child Guidance/Psychiatry
Elspeth Earle	Maidstone Health Authority
J S Edmondson	Grimsby Area Health Authority
Melonie Eldridge	Clermont Child Protection Unit
Michele Elliott	Kidscape
Kevin Epps	Glenthorne Youth Treatment Centre
Susie Essex	Bristol University
Sue Fallon	NSPCC
Jim Farebrother	Hereford & Worcs Probation Service
Alistair Findlay	Lothian Regional Council
Pauline Flavin	SACCS
Diana Foreman	Senior Solicitor, Kent Social Services Legal Team
Jane Fortin	Kings College London
Ena Fry	National Foster Care
Jean Gabbott	Strategy Group, Tower Hamlets Social Services
Tim Galton	Archway IT Centre
Pam Gillespie	Tayside Regional Council
Danya Glaser	Child Psychiatrist Guys Hospital
Angela Glendenning	Staffordshire Probation Service
Liz Goddard	Kent County Constabulary
David Gough	University of Glasgow
Mike Grady	Bradford Social Services
Helen Graham	Blackburn & Dist Children's Homes
Edwina Grant	Strathclyde Regional Council
Mary Groarke	Manchester Social Services
David Gurr	Assistant Director, Calderdale Social Services
B Gutteridge	Det Supt, West Mercia Constabulary
Val Haarbosch	Norfolk Social Services Dept
Gary Haigh	Det Chief Inspector, West Yorkshire Police
Dr H Hamid	Consultant Paediatrician, Peel House Community Unit
Vernon Hampson	Northampton Juvenile Liaison Bureau
Mary Hanley	Strathclyde Regional Council
Phil Hannan	The Children's Society
Paul Harnett	Insitute of Psychiatry
Hereward Harrison	ChildLine
Janet Harrison	Child Protection Adviser, Kent Social Services
Sheila Harvey	Sydney House Communities
Judith Harwin	Dept of Social Admin, London School of Economics
Phil Haslam	Buckingham Social Services
Lynda Henderson	Lancs Social Services Dept
Bill Hendley	Coventry Social Services
Tadeusz Heyda	Southwark Social Services
Chris Hickey	The Rainer Project
Anne Hignett	Child Protection, Greenwich Social Services
Dr Julie Hird	Clinical Psychologist, Forensic Psychology Service
Masud Hoghughi	Aycliffe Centre for Children
Alan Holden	
Judy Holloway-Vine	Ambervale Obs & Assessment Centre
Anne Hollows	National Children's Bureau
Anne Houston	ChildLine, Scotland
Elaine Howard	ChildLine
Philip Hudson	Deputy Director, North Tyneside Social Services
Doug James	Kettering Juvenile Liaison Bureau

Richard Jarrett	Cheshire Social Services
Carolyn Jones	
Charlie Jones	Juvenile Community Support Team
R H Kathane	Consultant Child Psychiatrist, Union Street Clinic
Judith Kettle	NCH
Diana King	Hampshire Social Services
Chris Kingham	NSPCC
Nicholas Kitchen	Worksop College Boarding School
Paul Kitchen	Wiltshire Social Services
Robert Lake	Director, Humberside Social Services
Chris Langford	Juvenile Justice Centre
Alison Leake	LB Merton Social Services
Linda Learney	SPO Sex Offenders Unit, Northumbria Probation Service
Shelley Lewis	Child Protection, Liverpool Social Services
Anthony Livesey	Child, Adolescent & Family, N Derbyshire Health Authority
Rachel Lahoup	Child & Family Therapy, Nottingham Health Authority
Sean Loughlin	Norfolk Social Services Dept
Stuart Lumsden	Strathclyde Regional Council
Jim Lyon	Strathclyde Regional Council
Dr Maclachlan	Community Child Health, Addenbrookes Hospital
R Macklin	DCI, Northamptonshire Police
Phil Madden	Avon Social Services
Tony May	Somerset Social Services
Rena McCarry	Strathclyde Regional Council
Gerry McGeoch	NCH
Roisin McGoldrick	Strathclyde Regional Council
Jim McInally	Strathclyde Regional Council
Peter Mckelvie	Hereford & Worcester Social Services
Prof.Sheila McLean	University of Glasgow
Margaret Mckinnon	Strathclyde Regional Council
K Measor	The Oaks Centre
Moyra Menzies	Strathclyde Regional Council
David Metcalfe	NCH
David Miller	Nottinghamshire Social Services
Ian Milner	Social Services Inspectorate
Peter Misch	Institute of Psychiatry
Elizabeth Monck	Institute of Child Health
P Montague	The Oaks Centre
S Morley	The Oaks Centre
Rod Morris	Mental Health Unit, St Lukes Hospital
Tony Morrison	NOTA
Mick Muir	Child Protection Manager, Tameside MBC
Elizabeth Mulley	Kent County Constabulary
Julie Murphy	Bury Social Services
Peter Murphy	Shropshire Social Services
John Newcombe	N Yorkshire Social Services Dept
Philip Noyes	NSPCC
Marie O'Brien	Blackburn & District Children's Homes
Alayne O'Connor	Gloucester Social Service Dept
Lynda O'Donnell	Tayside Police
Debbie O'Flynn	N Yorkshire Social Services Dept
Maureen O'Hara	Children's Legal Centre
Anne Olliver	Alternatives to Custody & Care
Deirdre Offord	Family Care
A P Orchard	Coxlease School
Beryl Otvos	LB Harrow Social Services
Paul Overton	Sheffield F & Cs
Susan Owen	Education/Juvenile Liaison, Wellingborough Liaison Bureau
Marcus Page	Clermont Child Protection Unit
Kyveilie Papas	West Lambeth Health Authority
Ian Partridge	N Yorkshire Social Services
V Pattison	The Oaks Centre
Neil Peaswick	Bedfordshire Social Services
Jill Pedley	Leicestershire Social Services
Barbara Peel	JP Magistrates Association
Kevin Perkins	Children's Psychiatric Unit

Carol Phaun	Strathclyde Regional Council
Frank Phelan	Hollybank F R C
Richard Pick	N Yorkshire Social Services Dept
Mark Platt	Portsmouth & SE Hants Health Authority
A G Plumtree	Association of Reporters – Children's Panel
K E Purser	Probation Officer, Juvenile Justice Unit
Meena Randhawa	PO Child Protection, Birmingham Action on Child Care
Phil Rayner	NSPCC
Brian Reed	Detective Superintendent, Wiltshire Constabulary
Linda Regan	Polytechnic North London
Howard Roberts	Child Psychiatrist, St Thomas Hospital
Morian Roberts	Child Psychiastrist, South Devon H/C Trust
Jean Robertson	SE London Probation Service
Christine Robinson	NCH
Anne Rogers	NSPCC
Kathy Rolph	Bloomsbury & Islington Health Authority
Clare Roskill	CCETSW
Olsen Samuel	Director Social Services, L.B. Haringey
Adam Sampson	Deputy Director, Prison Reform Trust
Donald Scott	Lothian Regional Council
Babs Seymour	Caldecott Community
Alison Seymour	ChildLine Midlands
Peggy Shaffter	Project Leader, Essex Social Services
Paul Sharkley	NSPCC
Peter Short	Mental Health Unit, NE Essex Health Authority
Viki Simpson	Southwark Social Services Dept
S Slavin	Hesley Group of Schools
A Smith	Grampian Police
Gerrilyn Smith	DoH Course Lecturer, Great Ormond Street Hospital
Lucille Smith	NSPCC
Marjorie Smith	Thomas Coram Foundation
Wendy Smith	Sandwell Social Services
Morven Sowerbutts	Social Worker, Cheshire Social Services
J Stafford	Greater Manchester Probation Service
Tony Stead	Hollybank F R C
Theresa Stephenson	Senior Social Worker, Fife Social Work Dept
Jenny Still	Gracewell Clinic
Gordon Stone	Kent Probation Service
Denise Stoneman	SE London Probation Service
Gillian Tagg	Mental Health Unit, Leeds Health Authority
Cathy Taylor	Tayside Health Board
G R Thompson	Senior Social Worker, LB Wandsworth Social Service
Prof. Thompson	University of Glasgow
L Thomson	Grampian Police
Jane Tunstill	NCVCCO
L Turnbull	Inspector, Humberside Police
Lesley Turner	Hollybank F R C
Thomas Tweed	Inspector, Bedfordshire Police
Tracey Vickers	Leicester Social Services
Anne Walsh	LB Newham Social Services
Derek Wardle	Derbyshire Probation Service
Dr Margaret West	Cheshire Health Authority
Rob West	The Rainer Project
Michael Wilkins	Lewisham & N Southwark CSA Team
Robert Wilkins	NHS Paxton House
David John Will	Lothian Health Board
Catriona Williams	Mid Glamorgan Social Services
Dick Williams	Archway I T Centre
Andrew Wilson	Strathclyde Regional Council
W Wood	LB Lambeth Social Services
Sue Woodcock	Barnardo's
Howard Woolfenden	Child Protection Team, Dudley Social Services
Shirley Wright	Blackburn & Dist Children's Homes
Ray Wyre	Gracewell Clinic
Michelle Young	N Yorkshire Social Services Dept
Dr H Zeitlin	Child Psychiatrist, Wesminster Children's Hospital